A Marian Devotional

Edward F. Garesché, S.J.

# A Marian Devotional

SOPHIA INSTITUTE PRESS®
Manchester, New Hampshire

*A Marian Devotional* is an abridged edition of *The Most Beloved Woman* (New York: Benziger Brothers, 1919). For this 2002 edition by Sophia Institute Press®, the chapter entitled "The Most Beloved Woman in Prophecy" from the original edition has been omitted, the chapter titles have been revised, and minor editorial revisions and Marian prayers have been included.

Sophia Institute Press®
Box 5284, Manchester, NH 03108
1-800-888-9344
www.sophiainstitute.com

*Nihil obstat:* Arthur J. Scanlan, S.T.D., *Censor Librorum*
*Imprimatur:* Joseph F. Mooney, V.G., Administrator of New York
New York, February 25, 1919

**Library of Congress Cataloging-in-Publication Data**

Garesché, Edward F. (Edward Francis), 1876-1960.
  A Marian devotional / Edward F. Garesché.
    p. cm.
  Abridged ed. of: The most beloved woman. 1919.
  Includes bibliographical references.
  ISBN 1-928832-47-4 (pbk. : alk. paper)
  1. Mary, Blessed Virgin, Saint — Prayer-books and devotions —
    English. I. Garesché, Edward F. (Edward Francis), 1876-1960.
    Most beloved woman. II. Title.
  BX2160.23 .G37 2002
  232.91 — dc21                                    2001007407

02  03  04  05  06  07  08  09  10  9  8  7  6  5  4  3  2  1

It was you, my earthly mother, who taught me to love my Mother in Heaven and, from your own goodness, helped me to understand the fairness and holiness of Mary. By your hands, then, I offer this book to her.

*To the Most Blessed Virgin Mary,*
*Queen of All Saints*

Editor's note: The biblical quotations in the following pages are taken from the Douay-Rheims edition of the Old and New Testaments. Where applicable, quotations have been cross-referenced with the differing names and enumeration in the Revised Standard Version, using the following symbol: (RSV =).

# Contents

⌒

*Biographical Note:*
Edward F. Garesché, S.J.

# Preface

These pages are not meant as a complete or systematic treatise on the Blessed Virgin. They do not seek to exhaust the inexpressibly rich and beautiful theme that they touch so occasionally and briefly. Rather, they are pious meditations on certain of the prerogatives and glories of the Mother of God. When we consider that the Blessed Mother is, after her divine Son, the loveliest object of human contemplation, it is rather strange that more has not been written in English in her praise. If this little book stirs a more ardent love of the holy Mother in its readers and makes them desire to read more Marian literature, it will have fulfilled its purpose.

And while offering this small and wilted flower at the shrine of the Mother of God, the writer hopes that some

future time may bring him the opportunity of making a
worthier tribute to the boast and glory of our mere human nature: the Most Beloved Woman, the dearest
Mother of God.

*A Marian Devotional*

## We are dear to
## the Most Beloved Woman

It is the blessed gift of every pure and holy woman to gather about herself the love of some devoted hearts. If her sphere is small, her true lovers will be few. If she is known far and wide, the circle will be larger, for her innocence and goodness will appeal to a greater number of loyal and impressionable hearts. But the circle of such devoted and unselfish worship can never be very wide, because the affection we speak of is not admiration or reverence or distant service; it is the sort of intimate, personal devotion that a son gives to his mother — a friend to his intimate friend.

True friendship cannot be maintained with a multitude. The constant give-and-take of benefits and love that it requires cannot extend beyond a certain few, or it would soon exhaust our limited powers. Friendship and devotion must be mutual to exist at all, and so even the purest and best of women gather to themselves in this intimate and personal way of which we speak only a few devoted friends and loved ones.

Yet, to every pure and womanly heart, these few loving friends, whether they be blood relatives, or brothers and sisters and sons and daughters of the soul, are inexpressibly dear. To help them and be aided by them, to confide in them and take their confidences, is the consolation of her life. Her loving solicitude goes out to them constantly, and she lives and plans and prays much more for her friends and unselfish loved ones than for any merely personal end. They are her other self, more than the half of her heart.

Such thoughts bring us a little nearer, it may be, to realizing one astonishing and singular privilege of the Most Blessed Virgin. All the noblest prerogatives of her sex have been unutterably deepened and widened for her, and so, too, has this dear privilege of drawing and holding to herself the purest love of hearts. That intimate and personal devotion, that tender love of sons and daughters for their mother, of brothers and sisters for their sister, of friends for a most dear friend, are all bestowed innumerable times over on God's dear Mother. The love that she possesses from devoted hearts is deeper, truer, and more enduring than any love of earth.

Indeed, the love we give to the Virgin Mary has borrowed the strength and fervor of every holy and unselfish human love. Men and women love Mary more because they love their mothers, sisters, and friends. When grown men pray to her, there rises in their hearts a sweet, half-conscious remembrance of their own dear mothers, and this fond memory lends a tenderness to the thoughts of her. She has drawn to herself the charm and endearing sweetness of the pure love of all other mothers. They die, and their love would pass and be forgotten, if the immortal motherhood of Mary did not draw to itself, and make perpetual, the strength and sweetness of the filial devotion of their sons and daughters.

Again, consider how the number of the devoted sons and daughters of our Blessed Lady exceeds the narrow circle of any other pure and holy woman's friends. When she declared, "All generations shall call me blessed,"[1] she might well have said also, "and beloved." It is a very

---

[1] Luke 1:48.

test of saintliness to be an ardent lover of God's Holy Mother.

The sweet name of Mary sings in the canticles of the Church, echoes in her liturgies, rings through all the exhortations of her saints, shines on her altars, and glitters on her banners. She is written into great literature, woven into tapestries, painted in glorious pictures, built into cathedrals, and sculpted in stone. The world is sown, thick as the skies with stars, with lovers of our Lady. Only think of the innumerable Catholic homes, scattered over the world, from the spot where you dwell to the uttermost borders of the earth. In every truly Catholic home, the holiest name of woman, the sweetest memory of woman, is the name and memory of Mary.

*Mary receives and returns the love of all hearts*

But it should stir our hearts still more to dwell on the worthiness and power of this sweet and holy Virgin to attract and repay such measureless devotion. Other women cannot have more than a very limited circle of true friends. The reason is, as we have said, that they cannot deal with more than a very few in the sweet give-and-take of confidence and affection that is the soul of friendship. But the Blessed Mother is as powerful as she is merciful and loving, as strong as she is holy and fair. The multitude of her sons and daughters does not confuse her, their endless petitions do not embarrass her, for she has unspeakable strength and power from God to be to all men truly a mother. The cries at her thousand shrines rise efficaciously to her great heart, which is made strong and tender to hear and grant them all. Our hearts soon weary of loving, because they are small and weak. The heart of Mary never wearies, because it was made by God Himself mighty and deep and wide to mother all mankind.

There are a thousand sweet consequences for each one of us from this blessed prerogative of Mary, of drawing to herself and repaying the intimate and personal friendship of all hearts. Not only are we most truly her friends and children, but she is truly our friend and Mother. We need never lack an intimate and devoted confidant, a tender consoler, or a compassionate and gentle advocate, so long as we have, all our own, the Blessed Virgin Mary.

When we feel utterly unworthy to approach her adorable Son, we may speak to Him through the heart of Mary. When we are disappointed in earthly loves, we may be very sure of meeting no sorrow or distress where no one ever sought comfort in vain or cried for aid without obtaining relief. When the death of others, whom we love, utterly casts us down, we may still turn to that immortal Mother over whom death has no empire, who has made us a place in her Son's eternal mansion, and keeps it for us — a true and faithful Mother, watching for our coming home.

Best of all, her love is not limited by our own hearts. Like all mothers, she loves us with a gratuitous and superabounding love — more than we ever shall deserve. This is the sweetest charm of friendship, of motherliness, and this exceeding love is found in no other woman's heart as it burns in the heart of Mary.

We should always think of the heart of our Blessed Mother as a heart intensely human in all that beseems a most pure and glorious humanity.

Our own natures are human indeed, but with a humanity spoiled by the sin of Adam. The humanity of our Blessed Mother is pure of all earthly stain. Yet none of the noble tenderness of our nature is foreign to her. She loves with a warm and generous emotion, and she desires our love in return as no other mother ever desired the love of her children.

# We are dear to the Most Beloved Woman

We should remember this whenever we think of our Blessed Lady. She looks to us for tenderness, gratefulness, and service in return for her own undying and unsleeping love. Although she is queen of angels and men, she is nevertheless still most truly a woman — the Woman of all women, who comes nearest in the tenderness of her mother's heart to the tenderness of the Heart of Christ.

Love and remembrance, reverence and service from the little circle of her friends and sons and daughters — these things are dear to the heart of every pure and holy woman. They are no less dear to the most pure heart of Mary.

⌒

### Mary desires our service

And while we honor her as our queen, let us not forget that she would have our service no less than our petitions. Our Mother wishes indeed that we should cry to her in our distress, but she desires also to have part in our joys, our hopes, and our successes. She wishes to be part of our life and to have her memory woven with our days, as through the life of a dutiful child there runs like a golden thread the love and service of mother.

# A Marian Devotional

To murmur occasional prayers, to think devoutly of her now and then, on some special feast — this is no fit service for a son or daughter of Mary. We must serve her as good and faithful children, with actions even more than words. We must guess her wishes and desires and must anticipate, with thoughtful love, what she would have us do for her dear sake.

It is not hard to guess what the Blessed Mother would have her children do at this special time. The world is fainting away for want of a love and knowledge of her adorable Son. The poor — for whom she must feel such special tenderness, because she was herself a daughter of the poor — are in sore need and are prey to proselytizers and fanatics of many kinds. Their little ones, growing up in godless surroundings, greatly lack instruction in the Faith. Truly, there is much work at hand to prove the truth of our tenderness and the sincerity of our devotion to the most lovable and loving of all women.

*Hail Mary, beloved Daughter of the Eternal Father!*
*Hail Mary, admirable Mother of the Son!*
*Hail Mary, faithful spouse of the Holy Spirit!*
*Hail Mary, my dear Mother,*
*my loving Mistress, my powerful sovereign!*
*Hail my joy, my glory, my heart and my soul!*
*Thou art all mine by mercy, and I am all thine by justice.*
*But I am not yet sufficiently thine.*
*I now give myself wholly to thee without*
*keeping anything back for myself or others.*
*If thou still seest in me anything that does not*
*belong to thee, I beseech thee to take it and*
*to make thyself the absolute Mistress of all that is mine.*
*Destroy in me all that may be displeasing to God,*
*root it up, and bring it to nought;*
*place and cultivate in me everything*
*that is pleasing to thee.*

St. Louis de Montfort[2]

[2] St. Louis de Montfort (1673-1716), founder of the Sisters of the Divine Wisdom and the Missionary Priests of Mary.

*Mary's heart is filled*
*with compassion for us*

It was worthy of the infinite tenderness of God to come down in visible flesh and share our sorrows with us. We find it easy to believe in the compassion of Christ on our miseries when we find Him suffering much greater things in His own innocent flesh. We know very well that the endurance of pain and sorrow brings a keener sympathy with others' sufferings, and so we carry our woes and griefs with complete confidence to Christ on the Cross. This is one of the many precious fruits of meditating on the Passion: it brings us a deeper, more trustful sense of our Lord's compassion.

For the same reason, it is good for us to dwell sometimes on the trials of our Blessed Mother. The thought of her afflictions will serve not only as an example to us, but also as a proof of her compassion. We shall go to her in our distresses with greater confidence if we realize that she can sympathize with us with a vivid and tender compassion because she also has suffered such things.

~

*Mary shared in Christ's sufferings*

Even if we had no positive testimony on the subject, we would have taken it for granted that our Blessed Mother suffered a great deal during her mortal life. First of all, she was the nearest to Jesus by nature, by love, and by sympathy; and all who are near to Jesus must drink deep of His cup of suffering. His symbol is the Cross, which stands for pain and contradiction; and who should be more deeply signed with the Cross of Christ than His own Mother?

But a still stronger reason for being sure that our Blessed Lady suffered beyond words during her mortal life is the unspeakable love and tender sympathy that bound her heart and soul to the adorable and agonized Heart and Soul of her Son. She was bound up with Him as no other mother was ever joined to child in sympathy and affection. Her heart, her feelings, her whole being

twined around His Heart and responded with inconceivable fidelity, sensitive sympathy, and perfect compassion to every tremor of pain or sorrow that shook the
fibers of His suffering Heart.

We suffer with those we love in proportion as we truly
love them and deeply realize their sorrow and affliction.
The love of Mary for her Son was deeper than the ocean,
and her comprehension of His sorrows was sharpened
by the threefold keenness of a mother's tenderness, a
virgin's pure devotion, and the mighty grace of God
that flooded her whole being with unbounded light.

She understood, then — this Mother of Sorrows —
as no other creature ever has understood, the sufferings
of the Word-made-flesh. She went far out with Him
into the dark spaces of loneliness and yearning where
His love pleaded for an ungrateful and betraying world.
She yearned with Him over the soul of every sinner who
ever flung away the friendship of God or spurned the
grace of the Blood of Christ. She pleaded with Him before the justice of the Father. She shuddered with Him
at the gulf of Hell and wept over the loss of souls.

I can still remember when first it dawned on me that
all the calm and holy hours of Christ's life were pierced
through with an all-but-unbearable agony because of the

sinfulness and ingratitude of men. I struggled against the thought with earnest determination. It was too pitiful to think that the Lamb of God was offered up in a life-long sacrifice by the passion and selfishness of men.

Yet who can doubt that Christ's entire life was full of the most acute mental suffering? For the sight of a world hardened and steeped in sin was ever before Him, and He knew the whole depth and breadth of human wickedness. How could the Infinite Holiness not suffer in the midst of such widespread evil? How could the Infinite Compassion not be distressed at so much misery?

No one has come so near to realizing and repaying the wounded tenderness and yearning love of the Heart of Christ as Mary. No one has gone so deep with Him into His desolation and sorrow, nor mourned so well with Him over His wayward race, as she who alone had no share or part in their transgressions. These two most innocent of the race of Adam have suffered together the most appalling penalty of sin.

⁓

*Mary was particularly sensitive to suffering*
Again, in dwelling on the sufferings of our Lady, we should remember that hers was a nature wonderfully

perfect, delicate, and sensitive to pain. It has been said of our Lord that His human nature was of all others most capable of intense suffering because it was most perfectly organized, most keen and delicate in all its faculties, and the more perfect the organization, the greater its capacity for suffering. This same reflection holds, with due allowance, for our Blessed Mother.

She, too, was, after our Lord, the flower of humanity. She was the perfect stem who bore the Flower of Judah. She, too, was admirably perfect in her sensibilities and powers. She, too, had an immense capacity for pain. Besides, we may be sure that her own mighty and continual prayer prevailed ever to deepen and widen her sympathy with her Son. For what is more natural to a mother's heart than to desire truly to suffer with her child?

Then — and this is an illuminating thought when we reflect on the sorrow of our Blessed Mother — the affliction and the grieving of the Sacred Heart of Jesus had a power to wound her heart beyond what any merely personal anguish could possess. She truly loved Him more than she loved herself — a triumph of grace and supernatural charity at which our poor and weak natures can but feebly guess. The love of Him utterly employed and, as it were, exhausted all the mighty powers of her heart, so that the center, so to speak, of her being was no longer within herself but in Him — in Him, her Creator, her Savior, and her Son.

She suffered more, then, this most loving Mother, in His woes and sorrows than she could have suffered in any merely personal afflictions of her own. The wounds that pierced His body in His awful Passion first agonized the deepest and dearest places of her heart.

That pale, silent woman, who walked so bravely near the bleeding form of Christ, when His disciples left Him, and who stood with such unfaltering strength near the Cross, where He hung dying, was really bearing a more intense grief, a more oppressive and excruciating agony, than any personal wounds or pain could ever have inflicted on her. She cared nothing for herself. She thought nothing of herself. Indeed, the sting of wounds, the throbbing of physical pain, would have been, in some sense, a relief for her, wounded as she was in the most tender and sacred sensibilities of her being.

She would have felt it a relief and joy to die for Him and repair in some sort our atrocious cruelty and hardness toward Him. She would have rejoiced, as the martyrs did in their prisons and in the flames, to ease her great love by some great physical sufferings. But the relief of physical pain was denied her, and she suffered only the agony, worse than death, of a mother who watches helplessly the anguish of her son.

Not lightly does the Church give to this Most Beloved Woman the name of Queen of Martyrs, for all other martyrs confessed their God in the anguish of physical agony and death, but the Mother of God died many times over in spirit, in that most extreme anguish which pierced her quivering soul and crucified her heart.

*Mary's great sufferings have*
*made her greatly compassionate*

With what complete and tender confidence, then, with what simple trust may we not seek the compassion of our Blessed Mother! Kind beyond conceiving, by nature and the grace of God, her heart has besides been made more tender still in the fiercest fire of tribulation. It has become more compassionate than any other merely human heart, by bearing more exquisite sorrows and experiencing more agonizing depths of pain. If any mother's heart knows compassion, or can feel for the needs of her children, it is the stainless heart of Mary.

Now and again, even in our ordinary days, we come upon some heroic woman who has borne the fierce trial of an excruciating sorrow and come forth from that fiery ordeal strengthened and purified. And what depths of human kindness and compassion — what strength and peace and tenderness such a proved soul displays toward those who seek her for consolation! Suffering, nobly borne, has some admirable virtue that ripens the better instincts of the heart as the summer heat ripens the grain.

If sorrow can do so much even for the lowlier daughters of Eve, what blessed fruits of tenderness and compassion have not her great dolors ripened for us in the heart of Mary?

Let us bring all our needs and griefs, then, with utter confidence to our most compassionate Mother. In all else, the heart of the Most Beloved Woman is the faithful mirror of the Heart of Christ.

Her compassion, too — deep, motherly, and tender — is nearest to the boundless tenderness and sweet compassion of the Word-made-flesh.

O Mother of Sorrows,
with strength from above
you stood by the Cross,
sharing in the sufferings of Jesus,
and with tender care you bore Him
in your arms mourning and weeping.

We praise you for your faith,
which accepted the life God planned for you.
We praise you for your hope, which trusted
that He would do great things for you.
We praise you for your love, in bearing,
with Jesus, the sorrows of His Passion.

Holy Mary,
may we follow your example
and stand by all our children
who need comfort and love.

Mother of God,
stand by us in our trials
and care for us in our many needs.
Pray for us now
and at the hour of our death. Amen.

~

## Mary has a motherly love for us

We are all, in the eyes of God, as little, helpless children, and we need a mother. He has considered our weakness and our want from the beginning and has provided for us the one elect and perfect woman who can be a mother to all mankind. Thus, in this, as in all things, the Infinite Mercy has had a care for our necessities. He made us and knows that we are weak and naked and poor, and that we want constant mothering.

True, we each have, when we are tiny babies, our own natural mother; but, despite the mighty instinct of motherhood that God has planted in every woman's heart, there are many mothers who have no skill to guard and train their children, others who are wicked and will not, and others still whom death prevents before they can accomplish what they would. For these neglected babies, God has given a universal Mother.

And we others, who have grown up in the shelter of a mother's love, whose youth was sanctified by that pure and hallowing influence, we also find, when we go out into the world, that we still need a mother. There remain in us, even until extreme old age, even until death, yearnings and weaknesses and needs for comfort and intercession that make us crave, unconsciously and blindly it may be, for some spiritual mothering.

It is befitting, therefore, that God, who has deigned to illustrate for us His own great love by comparing it to the love of a mother, should provide for all mankind by His omniscience and power a Mother great enough to cherish all her race and loving enough to give every mortal, without exception, the intimate care and personal affection of a mother.

⁓

*Mary attends to the needs of every person*

It was a task that only All-Wisdom could conceive and only Omnipotence could accomplish. Consider the unthinkable diversities of men. Remember the flowing millions that pervade the earth, swarming in every land, pouring from age to age in incessant and ever-changing variety, countless and bewildering, many as the sands of the seashore, different as the flowers of summer, with needs and aspirations and wants and cares that it would seem only the knowledge of God could compass and only the heart of God could pity or even understand.

What a more-than-angelic intelligence is needed to comprehend and to remember the needs and petitions of so many! What a more than seraphic love is required to intercede for the pardon and help of this clamorous and bewildering torrent of mankind, sweeping forever from the seething springs of birth to the misty ocean of death, pouring through so many channels, and filling the air with the voice of so many cries!

Can there be any woman, on earth or in Heaven, so wise that she can comprehend and keep in her mind the needs of so many souls, and so good and great of heart that she can mother, with individual and persistent care, these many needs that our littleness cannot even conceive or understand?

If we consider the nature of a mother's love, the marvel increases that any woman can be all mankind's true mother. A mother's love is extremely special, particular, and exclusive. Its very intensity, solicitude, and depth of

feeling confine it, for most women, to their own imme-
diate offspring, and we even find in a family of many
children that the mother's heart is sometimes too narrow to love them all equally, and what she gives in
strength of affection to one is in a certain sense taken
from another.

How can one woman, then, be a mother to all the
world? She needs a heart that is equal, in the capacity of
its comprehension, the tenderness of its care, and the
sublime and surpassing talent for loving, to all the
mothers' hearts of all the earth. She needs much more;
for whereas not all the mothers of the world really love
and cherish their children, this Mother of all mankind
must, out of her heart, supply for all the sad mothers
who are so only in name and have not a mother's heart.

Considering all these things, and striving to comprehend the vastness of the human race, its pitiful need,
and the meaning of a mother's love, we might have
questioned whether it was in the nature of things that
one woman could be mighty enough and kind enough
to take upon her sole self the task of mothering the
world and have a heart so wide as to embrace all mankind. But God has answered the question by making
such a woman and by giving her such a heart. And the

name of the woman is Mary, the Mother of God and all men's Mother.

⤳

*God enabled Mary's heart to love all persons*

God does all things easily, and the greatest to Him is even as the least. Otherwise we might have piously imagined that, in His planning of the universe, He dwelled longest, after the Heart of Christ, upon the heart of Mary. Her heart is the masterpiece of all creation, after the Heart of Christ. And it matters more to us than we ever realize, how perfect and complete God made the mother's heart of Mary.

Whenever God gives an office to anyone, He gives the talents and natural gifts that are needed for the perfect fulfillment of what He wishes. This is what we would expect from His wisdom and His goodness. Indeed, so true is it that God fits us specially for whatever task He vouchsafes to give us that when there is question as to whether a person has such and such a vocation — as, for instance, a vocation to the religious life — the first question to be asked is this: Has he the gifts of nature that are required to fulfill the duties of that state? For if God has not provided the gifts, it is usually clear that He does not give the calling. We may thus be sure that in ordaining the Blessed Virgin to be the Mother of all men, He has also given her a heart that fits her to be all men's true Mother.

How vast and deep are her affections, how sensitive her sympathy, how immense her compassion, and how prompt her kindness and her mercy! All generations have witnessed this when they have called her blessed, not only for the gifts she has received, but for the use she made of them. We can, therefore, sum up the greatness of the heart God gave her by saying that He made her heart to mother all the world. Then we may ponder for a lifetime on the meaning of these words and never exhaust their immense significance.

What a heart must be the heart of Mary! What words will bear the strain of striving to express the strength and sweetness of that heart, and not break down and lose their significance because they are bidden to say things inexpressible beyond their reach? When, in the light of prayer, the saints have been so happy as to fathom in some degree the heart of Mary, their joy has found expression, not in words, but in speechless ecstasy. It is her heart that has made her mightiest among all the sons and daughters of Adam — greatest of all mere creatures, and most prevailing both with God and with men.

The power of our human nature is in the heart. The will with its handmaids, the affections, rules all creation and is mighty with both earth and Heaven. More than by interest or by fear, the world is ruled by love, and it was this consideration that moved the Son of God, when He set out to conquer the world perfectly and forever, to put aside the glory of His divinity and the splendor of His riches and come among us as one of us, drawing to Himself all Adam's children with the cords of Adam.[3] So the strength and sweetness of her motherly heart are the great sources of Mary's power over her children. She rules us as a mother, by the love of her heart.

☙

*We come to know Mary by*
*pondering the qualities of her heart*

The history of men is in great measure the history of their hearts. If we know anyone's heart, we know also his inmost history. But in the case of most human beings, it is exceedingly difficult to obtain a knowledge of

---

[3] Osee 11:4 (RSV = Hos. 11:4).

their hearts. The heart is interior, secret, and deep; and it manifests its mysterious workings only by those exterior actions which it is sometimes so hard to interpret rightly and which disclose so grudgingly the very thing perhaps that we most need to know to form a just and fair notion of the heart. This is true even of the simplest and least educated of mankind, and as one ascends in the scale of intellect and training, it becomes increasingly difficult to gain an intimate knowledge of the heart. The men and women who have left the greatest impress on history are often little known to us, because we cannot fathom the deep recesses of their hearts. The secret of their power is somewhere contained in the hearts that they kept concealed. We can never comprehend them now, because they have left behind them no story of their heart.

On the other hand, even those most gifted in self-expression, the poets and the artists who were able with keen power to set their hearts out to be seen by men, have not succeeded in giving us all we need to know their hearts intimately, because, for one, they did not know themselves. In the moments of supreme inspiration in which they conceived their masterpieces of expression, they were rapt out of themselves and built better than they knew. But the secret of their hearts is hidden from us. Indeed, it would be rash for us to think that we know them at all, save only as their works tell us of a passing mood or an incidental thrill of beauty. The secrets of their hearts have died with them and are lost to us.

But, most happily, and in some sense amazingly, it is not so with the heart of the Most Beloved Woman, who is our Mother. Although we have only one small poem of her composing — the *Magnificat*[4] — and only a few words and actions of her life recorded in the Sacred Scriptures, we know more, and more surely, concerning the heart of the Blessed Mother than about that of any character in history, save only our Blessed Lord. For by thinking all that the heart of Mary should be, we know at once all that she truly is in her most pure and blessed heart. She was full of grace on earth, and is so in Heaven. She never in any respect whatever departed by a hair's breadth from the law of God. She is the ideal of Christian goodness, of perfect motherliness, of holy virginity, of perfect charity toward God and men. To know what her heart was and is, we have therefore only to ask ourselves what it should be.

[4] Luke 1:46-55.

# A Marian Devotional

We could spend many happy hours thinking with assurance and delight of the heart of the Blessed Mother. What love of God is there, and what tenderness for ourselves! Think of the goodness, the piety, the faithfulness of a mother's heart, and then strive to measure the affection toward you in particular that glows in the heart of your heavenly Mother. Strain your conceiving to picture her care over you and the interest she takes in all your affairs, the attention she gives to your prayers, the solicitude with which she watches over all your ways, and then think to yourself that you have fallen far short of doing justice to the heart of that most perfect and faithful Mother.

We owe gratitude to God for many things. We can never understand, much less repay, His bounties to us. It will be one of the keen joys of Heaven to acknowledge and thank Him more and more for the goodness He has showered upon us. And in that clear and joyful revelation, when we see with God's eyes and are enlightened with His understanding, one of our most exquisite delights will be to comprehend in our measure the heart of our Mother, and to render to God eternal praise for this, after His own divine Son and the Holy Spirit, the greatest of His gifts to men.

O Virgin Immaculate,
Mother of God and my Mother,
from your sublime heights,
turn your eyes of pity on me.
Filled with confidence in your goodness
and knowing full well your power,
I beg you to extend to me your
assistance in the journey of life,
which is so full of dangers for my soul.
In order that I may never be a slave
of the Devil through sin, but may ever
live with my heart humble and pure,
I entrust myself wholly to you.
I consecrate my heart to you forever,
my only desire being to love your divine Son, Jesus.
Mary, none of your devout servants
has ever perished;
may I, too, be saved. Amen.

St. Ephraem of Edessa[5]

---

[5] St. Ephraem of Edessa (c. 306-373), deacon and Doctor.

## We are the recipients
### of God's gifts to Mary

Christmastime is a season of gifts. It should be also a time of earnest gratitude. On that great feast we commemorate the supreme gift of the Godhead to our human nature, in the Incarnation. We would do well to try to realize thankfully how much God gives us when He gives us Jesus and Mary.

It is said — you have heard it often — that the whole universe of God is so delicately linked and welded together, that whatever touches the tiniest part affects in some way the entire whole. A step on a grassy meadow sends a thrill to the farthest star!

Now, if this is true in the world of matter, it is tenfold true in the world of spirit. We are all members of a harmonious and delicately linked and welded system, and the good or evil of one of us reacts on the welfare of us all.

Men often go to Heaven or to Hell together and hand in hand. The influence of one of us on the other is measurable only by God. If you prayed more and lived better, your neighbor would be heartened to follow, and God would give him more grace for your sake. Indeed, our acts are as far reaching as the world of souls. Souls in China are better off, or worse off, according as you have prayed for or forgotten them. Even the joy of the angels is in some way increased by your good actions. Your goodness or your wickedness delights or grieves the very Heart of Christ Himself.

We matter tremendously, then — we little-seeming mortals — to one another. We give and take example, influence, and intercession. And it follows from this mutual influence that God's gifts to each one of us are in some sort given to us all.

This is true even in the intellectual order. The fiery passion and the swift, tremendous power of creative imagination that God gives to geniuses and poets enrich the whole world with noble and imperishable works. But in the order of grace, it is doubly true that God's

# We are the recipients of God's gifts to Mary

gifts to one are gifts to all. Every saint has left the whole world a better place than he found it. His prayers have saved and his example has leavened numbers of men. The graces that God gives us are never for ourselves alone; they are to have a wider influence than for our own perfection merely. We never become better ourselves without bettering someone else as well.

Pondering on this truth will bring us to realize how kindly and generously God has dealt with us through the ages, in raising up for us a host of saints. We are the heirs of those great servants of God. We enjoy the fruits of their sufferings, the benefits of their prayers, and the help of their intercession. They have blazed a path wherein we may follow. God's gifts to them have worked for our sanctification too; His favors to them have also been favors to us.

⌒

*God has enriched us with*
*the gifts of Jesus and Mary*

These thoughts prepare us to appreciate somewhat more deeply (there are depths beyond depths of thankfulness that we can never fathom) the unthinkable kindness that God has done to us in enriching beyond all measure the sacred humanity of Christ and the pure heart of His Most Beloved Mother. He has indeed given them incomparable gifts, but they themselves are His gifts to us. Every gift of God to the divine humanity, every fullness of grace that He poured into the brimming chalice of Mary's soul, has been the cause to us of unspeakable blessings. The fullness of their holiness redounds to our sanctification. They are made great and holy, not only for their own sake, but for the sake of all mankind.

This truth is made clearest when we consider the adorable humanity of Christ. He is the author of all grace, and its springhead. In creating that perfect humanity, and ordaining that it should be from the first instant united to the Word of God, the heavenly Father gave us our High Priest and our Victim — the Savior and Redeemer of us all. Through that individual human nature, the Word linked His adorable person with all humanity, and although it may be said of only one man that He is also the eternal God, we may each say that our human nature has been honored above all the angelic choirs by being assumed by the Eternal Word.

Thus, the supreme gift of God to humanity is a gift to every one of us, and all the stupendous favors that were

## We are the recipients of God's gifts to Mary

heaped on that human nature by consequence of its assumption by the Word were in a true sense given to us all. It was for us, for each of us, that the Word became flesh. It was for us that He was made the Firstborn of the children of God and dwelt among us.

This should form a subject of long and loving meditation for us, during the days that follow Christmas, as we tenderly recur in thought to the sweet and tiny Baby on the bosom of His Mother. He Himself is the supreme Gift of God. But every good and perfect gift that God's boundless love lavished and heaped on His human nature was but another gift bestowed on us. We also are the beneficiaries of every prayer that stirred His lips. We are the heirs of all His burning love, His prayers and merits and sufferings. The mark of all our sins is on Him. But on us is the mark of all His holiness!

When we turn from the Divine Baby to look upon the gentle Mother, we should strive to realize how all the gifts God heaped upon her great and holy heart were also bounties to ourselves; for as in Jesus He was preparing a Savior and a Brother for all men, so in Mary He was making for us all a Mother. After Christ, she is God's greatest gift to us. Each gift of God to her was given through her to all humanity.

# A Marian Devotional

It is said that God's greatest gifts are His most universal ones. In the physical order, the air, the earth, the sky, life, and in the spiritual order, grace, Heaven, and the love of God are offered to all men. So, too, these most perfect gifts of God's creation — the sacred brotherhood of Christ, the holy motherhood of Mary — are offered with supreme generosity to all mankind.

⁓

*We receive the gifts of Jesus and Mary*
*according to our free choice*

But it depends on our own zeal, fervor, and goodwill whether these gifts of God shall come to us in greater or in less perfection. The Child appeals to us; the Mother smiles on us. They besiege our hearts with gentle violence to follow them along the way of purity, holiness, self-sacrifice, and the surpassing love of God. They are not respecters of persons. It matters not to Jesus and to Mary that we are poor, despised, forgotten of the world; they still invite us to their intimate friendship and call us to their fellowship and service. Rather, they choose the poor and the forsaken lot as they did in Nazareth. But it rests with our own free choice to take part with them or not.

# We are the recipients of God's gifts to Mary

We must all become poor in spirit to follow the Child and His Mother. Their love is as free and universal as the air, as generous as the sun, as wide as the earth. What part we have in them depends on our own choosing, on the free inclination of our will. Even of the sun, air, and earth a man cannot always have as he chooses. But in Jesus and in Mary, in the Heaven He wins for us and in the grace she conveys to us, in the example He affords us and in the intercession she bestows on us, we can partake as widely as we choose.

There are no limits to God's power; there are no bounds to the good gifts we may have from Jesus and from Mary, save our own free will.

The tales of the East are full of the magnificence of those opulent monarchs who dealt about to their subjects the overflowing riches of their barbaric pearls and gold. Their own sweet will was the only limit to their bounty. Their treasuries were inexhaustible — full of the savings of their nation for century after century. They gave a province as though it were a field — a king's ransom as though it were a bauble.

But there came to the East a King who outdid in wealth and generosity the wildest dreams of these spendthrift kings. He promised each of His subjects a kingdom. His bounty was confined, not by His own sweet will, but by the will of anyone who should beseech Him. He dared to say (as even the richest of those lords of earth had never ventured), "Ask and you shall receive, seek and you shall find, knock and it shall be opened unto you"[6] — an appalling promise, and one that is possible to omnipotence alone. Because Christ is the Eternal Truth, He meant this promise most sincerely. Since He is the Eternal Faithfulness, He will fulfill it to the letter. We may have as great a part in Jesus and Mary as we will ask of them.

Of course, we must ask not with our lips only, but with our mind and our heart. We must truly will to have a part in Jesus and Mary, and the greatness of our part in them will depend on the earnestness and sincerity of our will.

We must take them as they are and desire to be like them. They are poor in spirit and suffering in body. They are chaste and meek and kind and lowly, and they hold the world as nothing in comparison with the love of God and the kingdom of Heaven. When we desire sincerely to have a part with Jesus and Mary, we must

[6] Cf. Matt. 7:7.

sincerely desire these things also. We must desire to be unworldly, to love our fellowmen — not some of them merely, as the pagans do, but all of our fellowmen. We must desire to take God's part against the world, to suffer persecution for justice's sake, to bear wrongs patiently, to be peacemakers, and to be clean of heart. And we must will all of these things with a true, sincere, actual, honest purpose, not merely with the impulse of transient feeling or with the passing sigh of devotion.

It is the will that God looks to when we pray. We must ask with all our will to receive a part in Jesus and Mary. We must keep a steady and constant will to retain our part in them.

But it is worth our while — immensely worth our while — to go to any pains or make any sacrifice to have a part with Jesus and Mary. For, little and slight as they seem — outcasts in the stable of Bethlehem, forsaken of the world — and great and powerful as the world seems that has cast them out of its inns and will not take part with them, Jesus and Mary are strong and mighty and enduring, and the great world is weak and fickle and passes like a dream. We may gain a great part in the world, and within fifty years, we shall find that the world has slipped from us, and our hands will be empty, but the part we gain in Jesus and Mary we shall possess as long as God is God.

⸙

*Through us, others may*
*receive the gifts of Jesus and Mary*

Not for our own selves only should we desire to have a great part in Jesus and Mary. For as they are God's greatest gifts to us and all of God's gifts to them redound to our profit, so may we become gifts and blessings of God to our fellowmen, and all God's graces given to us will redound to our brothers' benefit as well. Just in proportion as we become like Jesus and Mary, so shall we be able to give to other men and women a part in Jesus and Mary, to win the world to them by our example, and help it by the graces we merit.

To a generous soul, this should be one of the strongest motives to strive for a great part in Jesus and Mary. We must become like them before we can lead others to their feet. We must know the way ourselves to the stable at Bethlehem before we can bring others there. The shepherds and the Magi went first themselves before they spread the good tidings abroad. When a man finds a great treasure, he may indeed call his neighbors to share it with him, but he will first take a share himself. If he does not care to possess it, his neighbors will never believe that he has found anything worth caring about.

The love of God, then, and the right love of ourselves, and the love of our neighbor — these three loves, which embrace all worthy love, urge us most strongly to gain a mighty part in Jesus and Mary. Let us think these thoughts over many times during the Christmas season, and at every sacred season. Let us haunt with a holy longing the little cave of Bethlehem.

We need not speak many words nor say striking or moving things to Jesus and Mary. The desires of our hearts will speak for us. We need only let our true wills yearn long and earnestly to have a great and lasting part in the Child and His Mother.

*You are all fair, O Virgin Mary.*
*You never knew the stain of sin.*
*You are the glory of Jerusalem,*
*You, the joy of Israel,*
*You, the great honor of our people,*
*You, the advocate of sinners.*
*O Mary, Virgin most prudent,*
*O Mary, Mother most merciful,*
*Pray for us.*
*Intercede for us with our Lord,*
*Jesus Christ.*

## Mary teaches us
## to fix our gaze on Jesus

Not long ago, on the train, I chanced to see a mother with her baby in her arms. It was beautiful to mark the intense affection of her look as she gazed at the tiny face. Her whole soul was in her eyes. Then I thought of the unwearying devotion with which this mother's eyes would follow the growing child through all his years. She would watch every slight action, notice every sign of growth or change. Nothing that concerned her child would ever be indifferent to her, for this was her very son, dearer to her than her own life.

So I was enabled, seeing the rapt worship of this mother's eyes, feebly to conjecture how the eyes of the Most Beloved Woman fed upon her Baby as He lay in her arms, as weak and unregarded of the world as this small baby before me.

How well the Virgin Mother watched her Son! Nature and grace were so perfect and so admirably blended in her! The very maternal tenderness that fastened her eyes on Him, and made her heart beat faster for every budding charm that the days unfolded in His tiny face, was a source of grace to her. For to watch Jesus and imitate Him is the sum and epitome of all the wisdom of the saints, and who would ever watch Him so nearly or so well as this Most Beloved Woman? She was His Mother and His Daughter. She watched Him with the all-observant eyes of a mother and imitated Him with the fidelity of a dutiful child.

*Mary fixed her heart on Jesus amid all her tasks*

We may in fancy steal reverently in upon one of those peaceful days of which there were so many at Nazareth. The quiet morning has seen that dutiful housewife going through all her lowly tasks with the diligence of an angel and the love of a seraph — her body most active in God's outward service, her soul entirely intent on His interior love and adoration.

# Mary teaches us to fix our gaze on Jesus

Now the poor place is swept and garnished, the water jars are filled from the well, the floors and the walls shine with cleanness, the poor sticks of furnishings are ranged duly in decent order in the room.

And all the while, as her busy hands ply their task — O most admirable work-woman, sweet dignifier of the toil of millions of Eve's poor daughters! — the Mother's eyes have been on her Son. She has the mother's art of watching Him at all times, anywhere, in any occupation. Her eyes turn to Him, as certain flowers seek the sun, with a wistful, tender, thirsty fondness that drinks Him in, whenever she can steal an instant glance from the work her hands are doing. And in those brief instants when her tasks take her from the Presence, the eyes of her heart fix themselves with even greater intentness on the Son of her heart and the Father of her soul.

Her work to her is Jesus; her rest is Jesus. The quiet world and soft sky, the voices of the birds, the mild looks of little flowers, the lambs, the sheep that pass her doorway, the green hollow of the hills around Nazareth, the wistful distances that stretch away toward His town of Bethlehem and His city of Jerusalem, and the very round circle of the world that He has planned and made all cry and whisper and sing to her, "Jesus, Jesus," the livelong day, and day after day, from morning to sunset. The stars of heaven spell His name across the firmament. Her eyes seek only those shining mysteries to be reminded of His power and glory. Their glance hastens back to where the Baby is sleeping on her bosom, to read His gentleness and love.

Always, at all hours, for years upon years, the Most Beloved Woman had before her eyes — mother's eyes — the great object lesson. She saw open before her, in the very flesh, the textbook of holiness and perfection. And she studied Him, not only with her mother's eyes, but with her mother's heart.

We ourselves may well yearn, with the most intense desire, to have been given one glance at that heavenly Child. The very look of Him had an almost sacramental efficacy to pour the grace of God into our soul. One such glance would burn itself with a sweet pain into our memory and set us yearning for the everlasting look we shall fix on Him in Heaven. Yet how poor and weak is our devotion beside the motherly and virginal love that kept the eyes of Mary on the Word-made-flesh. She studied Him with her mother's heart.

For sympathy and comprehension, there is no equal to a mother's love. The look she bends on her son is edged with a twofold keenness of comprehension: her yearning affection and the resemblance between her own heart and her child's. Her love makes her desire to comprehend him. His likeness to her makes comprehension easy and deep. He has inherited from her everything but his soul, and even his soul, profoundly affected by its union with the body, becomes by that very fact attuned to hers. This wonderful thing, true of all sons and mothers, was especially true of this Mother and her Child. For she was His only parent on earth. She was His only tie with the children of Adam. All the resemblances that linked His human nature with His race came to Him through her pure self. Never was there closer resemblance between son and mother than this Most Beloved Woman bore to her Son, who is God.

So her heart was endlessly competent to study and understand Him. She could conjecture, with the swift sureness of a mother, the motions of that tiny Heart which is greater than the earth, and hear, in deepest rapture, the wordless language that spoke to her out of His infant silences. One look from Him had an eloquence to her that almost overpowered her heart, so rich and various were its messages. She understood her Son perfectly and imitated Him completely. This is the whole story of the Most Perfect Woman who ever lived on earth.

*Mary learned from Jesus*
*the grandeur of little things*

What sets us wondering most is the extreme simplicity of saintliness as practiced by Jesus and Mary. It does not consist in multiplied devotion, although all the great devotions of the Church were practiced sublimely in that little household — the devotion to the Sacred Heart, to Mary, and to Joseph. It does not lie in perplexing and head-fatiguing observances, or in agonized self-examination, or in terrific penances, although the Blessed Mother was the soul of fidelity, humility, and mortification. But her sanctity, like that of her Son, was the perfection of fidelity and love, in the small things of every day. She studied the God in flesh from His tender babyhood and discerned that His whole will was to do the will of His Father in Heaven. She learned that to be wrapped in swaddling clothes, when the Father willed it, might be raised by the intenseness of the heart's love to as great and meritorious an action as to lie meekly upon the Cross when He decreed.

## Mary teaches us to fix our gaze on Jesus

She learned to despise the wisdom of the world. The world, if it had known that God was on earth, would have called on Him to walk abroad in majesty and power, glorifying Himself above the princes of earth. It would have bidden Him lose no time in setting about His career and establishing His kingdom. Mary saw her Son peacefully delay for nearly all His lifetime, leading His carpenter's life, a laboring man, straining at the coarse wood with tired muscles, and gripping with His calloused hands the rude tools for hewing and sawing, hacking and shaping the plows and benches of the poor.

She saw the Almighty use His human strength to weariness, in the most obscure work that He could find in Israel. The striplings of the great families of Judah were crowding the schools of the law, to become scribes and Doctors in Israel. Christ, the Son of God, spent His youth toiling like Adam, and watched and loved by Mary.

She learned the greatness of little things. When He came in from His rough work, His hands soiled with it, His body tired with it, the sweat of toil on His forehead, where the majesty of God abode almost visibly, her heart must have leaped, again and again, with a wonder that no use or custom could allay. She knew so well who

## A Marian Devotional

He was that lived under this rough garb of a peasant of Palestine. She realized, with a dizzy clearness of realization, who this was, what Person looked through these calm eyes and spoke with these parched and sun-burned lips. From long and loving meditation, the keen splendor of the Divinity, that Eternal Wonder, that exquisite Perfection, that infinite Reality who is God shone on her soul through the thin veils of flesh. The keenness of her mother-eyes almost pierced through into the Divinity. She almost realized, even in the flesh, the sweetness of the Look that is Heaven.

And this Person, this Presence, this Awe and Splendor, had been all the morning about what task of tremendous import and majesty? What had this heavenly Wayfarer found to do that was worth His tremendous overleaping of all the choirs and thrones and principalities of Heaven? He had come forth from inaccessible light and traveled the immeasurable distance from the infinite to the finite, to find what godlike task for His human hands to do? Even her comprehending heart must have fainted to conceive it. He had been toiling all morning and for many mornings, in the most obscure place of the most despised nation of the world, doing work that would not overtax the mind or skill of the simplest and meanest of day laborers. He was doing His Father's will.

It was a strange and heavenly wisdom that Mary gathered, watching her Son's hidden life of toil and lowliness. It was a new model of holiness and fidelity that Son displayed, day by day for thirty years, before His Mother's comprehending and adoring eyes!

Dearly beloved Mother, grant,
if it be possible,
that I may have no other spirit
but thine to know Jesus
and His divine will;
that I may have no other soul but thine
to praise and glorify the Lord;
that I may have no other heart
but thine to love God with a love
as pure and ardent as thine.
I do not ask thee for visions, revelations,
sensible devotion, or spiritual pleasures.
It is thy privilege to see God clearly; it is
thy privilege to enjoy heavenly bliss;
it is thy privilege to triumph gloriously in Heaven
at the right hand of thy Son and to hold
absolute sway over angels, men, and demons;
it is thy privilege to dispose of all the gifts of God,
just as thou willest.

Such is, O heavenly Mary, the "best part,"
which the Lord has given thee and
which shall never be taken away from thee —

and this thought fills my heart with joy.
As for my part here below,
I wish for no other than that which was thine:
to believe sincerely without spiritual pleasures;
to suffer joyfully without human consolation;
to die continually to myself without respite;
and to work zealously and unselfishly for thee
until death as the humblest of thy servants.
The only grace I beg thee to obtain for me
is that every day and every moment of my life
I may say, "Amen — so be it" to all that
thou didst do while on earth;
"amen — so be it" to all that
thou art now doing in Heaven;
"amen — so be it" to all that
thou art doing in my soul,
so that thou alone mayest
fully glorify Jesus in me
for time and eternity. Amen.

St. Louis de Montfort

## Mary leads us to
## choose freely the path of goodness

We weak and sinful mortals find it very hard to value aright the perfect and excellent virtue of Jesus and Mary. Our days are spent in wars with foes within and outside of us, and we cannot imagine their perfect mastery of their hearts. Our lives are a series of fallings and risings, of good resolves and inadequate fulfillments, and so it is impossible for us to understand the calm, strong course of their even and flawless virtue. We go about, even the heroes among us, with many a scratch and scar, to tell of the varying fortune of battles, and so we come in time almost to measure virtue by wounds.

All of the conflicts of Jesus and Mary were glorious victories that left them clean of any scars, and such

superhuman sinlessness tempts us half to doubt the real-
ness of their conflicts and to underestimate the glory of
their victories.

We are like those men who live in constant bicker-
ings and always sleep with weapons within grasp of their
fingers. Their battles are written all over their scarred
and mutilated bodies. How can they appreciate the
valor of the civilized soldier, who goes through long
campaigns and does not bear a single mark of strife?

This is a great pity and loss for us, not to realize the
splendid virtue of these two perfect models of mankind.
For the truth is that Jesus and Mary were not only the
most perfect of all human beings, but they were also the
most deeply tried and solidly proven of all heroic souls.
Their stainless innocence and most splendid sanctity
were not the guarded goodness of a child in his father's
house. They were the tried worth of a hero of many
wars, who is still so expert of arm, so dauntless and reso-
lute of will, as to beat back a thousand fearful enemies
without sustaining a solitary wound.

Let us think lovingly for a moment of the virtue of
Mary. For, as she is the perfect reflection of the virtue of
her holy Son, so, in speaking of her, we shall be telling
His glories, too. And, being a reflection, her goodness is

less blinding and more intelligible than His. Our astronomers study the sun's bright disk through darkened glass when they cannot bear to turn their eyes on the burning orb itself.

First of all, our Blessed Mother had not, it is true, the fierce internal wars and struggles to contend with that vex our flesh and spirit since the sin of Adam. She did not sin in Adam, and so she was spared those shameful temptations, those interior rebellions that torment most of mankind. Besides, it was not fitting that God's most pure Mother should suffer the indignity of such assaults of Hell. But this exemption from the rebellions of the flesh does not diminish the pure glory of the Blessed Mother.

We grow so used, as we have said, to measuring virtue by the difficulty of our conflict to preserve it that we cannot understand how supreme holiness can exist without temptation. But we must remember that temptation and trial only manifest virtue; they do not create it.

⸆

*Mary's will was perfectly united with God's*

The Blessed Virgin was prepared, in heart and will, for even the fiercest temptation. Her soul was so perfect in purity, so holy, that all the storms of Hell that might have dashed against it would never have shaken or dismayed her. Her soul was like the strong man armed, of whom the Gospel speaks, keeping his court in peace because he is strong.[7] Virtue and holiness depend on the will — that kingly faculty of choosing that alone determines our merit or our sin. The will of Mary was inviolably turned to God. The strong, pure, tranquil current of her desires flowed to the biddings of His grace, as the tides of ocean rise and fall and follow the drawings of the moon. Her mind, her heart, her whole being were ruled by the serene and constant power of her will, and that will answered to the last and least impulse of the grace of God.

With such a will, she was perfect and heroic in every act of her life, as God had disposed it for her, free from the rebellions of the flesh. With such a will, she would have walked unharmed through any fire of tribulation.

With ourselves, interior temptations have two great purposes in God's plan: to prove our virtue and to keep us humble. The virtue of Mary needed no such test, for her will constantly cleaved to God with its entire being.

[7] Luke 11:21.

Her humility needed no such stay, because she was the lowliest of God's creatures. Unless she had been supremely humble, she would surely have slipped and fallen from her dizzy height — dizzier by far than that which turned the head even of Lucifer, a prince of God's most excellent angels, and sent him falling lightning-like to Hell.

There is another aspect to our Blessed Mother's freedom from those temptations which spring from our own corruption. Even had she not been exempt from these by God's special favor, she would have fought them off bravely by the spotless innocence of her own upright will. There are some, even among our fallen race, whose pure wills and careful lives preserve them wonderfully from temptations and sins. To avoid every slight stain of half-deliberate sin is impossible, unless we have a special privilege from God, such as He gave to the Virgin Mary. But the vigilance of the pure will of the saints can so curb and guard the wayward impulses of our nature, that, as was said of St. Bonaventure,[8] they seem hardly to have sinned in Adam, so faultless are their lives. Who

---

[8] St. Bonaventure (1221-1274), Franciscan mystical theologian, scholastic, writer, bishop, and Doctor.

can doubt that such a heroism of patient conflict waited ready, if there had been any need, in the Immaculate Heart of Mary?

What has been said should banish the fallacious thought that her freedom from interior rebellions lessens the glory of the virtues of the Blessed Mother of God and men. But when we come to speak of her exterior trials, a very similar difficulty suggests itself.

No one can doubt that the Blessed Mother was sorely tried by many exterior afflictions. The prophecy of Simeon pointed out to her a path of piercing sorrow.[9] With her divine motherhood came the awful and dread vocation to be the Mother of the Crucified, and every sword that pierced the Heart of Jesus wounded most deeply her most tender of mother's hearts.

But when we think of the sorrows of Mary, an uncomfortable question may arise in our minds. She was indeed the Queen of Martyrs, the most afflicted of all women. She bore with supreme goodness and patience supreme trials and anguish. But had she not the plenitude of God's mighty grace? Her glory is indeed above all conceiving. But is her merit so great as it seems? Had

[9] Cf. Luke 2:34-35.

she not the fullness of God's grace within her, so that it was impossible for her to be anything but perfect, heroic and sublime?

⁀

*Mary's goodness sprang from her free will*

There is a deadly fallacy here that we must utterly uncover. It is the old error of Luther: that God's grace supplants and overpowers the freedom of the human will.

Grace is a mystery. So is the freedom of man's will. We shall never quite comprehend the great and evident truth that we are free to do good or evil as we choose. Neither can we understand how this freedom of our human will can harmonize with God's utter omnipotence and with the efficacious power of His grace to rule our souls.

It is with this truth as with so many evident facts of nature. We know, we are sure, but we cannot understand. For a hundred thousand years, so astronomers tell us, the earth has been straining swiftly toward the sun. For a hundred thousand years, it has been urging its way off into space. The resultant of these two mighty forces keeps the huge bulk of earth in its orbit, but what these powers are, or how they grip the stony substance of the world, no man can entirely comprehend.

It is so with mysteries. We know the facts, but we cannot fully explain them. They pass beyond the vision of our mind. So we know most surely that God's grace, omnipotent as it is, leaves the human will truly and actually free.

This is of Faith — and it adds an immense glory to the life of our Blessed Mother. The great light and warmth of God's grace in her mind and heart did not take away her free will; they only strengthened, enlightened, and exalted it.

If she had sinned, with that light, that sweetness, that vigor in her soul, she would have sinned indeed like Lucifer. But when she chose, day by day, to do the perfect will of God; when she watched for every motion of God's grace, and perfectly fulfilled it; when she turned from all allurements of self and the world and chose always what God willed, it was not with a blind and necessary service.

It was the free, glorious, and consummate faithfulness of the handmaid of the Lord that crowned all the gifts of nature and grace that God had showered upon her. It was the eager and mighty virtue of her will that made

her the Perfect Woman, most worthy of all God's creatures to be His Mother, who summed up all His life in
this one perfect word: "My food is to do the will of Him
who sent me, that I may perfect His work."[10]

[10] Cf. John 4:34.

Most holy Virgin,
who wast pleasing to the Lord
and became His Mother,
immaculate in body and spirit,
in faith and in love,
look kindly on the wretched
who implore thy powerful patronage.
The wicked serpent, against whom
was hurled the first curse,
continues fiercely to attack and ensnare
the unhappy children of Eve.

Do thou, then, O Blessed Mother,
our queen and advocate,
who from the first instant of thy conception
didst crush the head of the enemy,
receive the prayers which,
united with thee in our single heart,
we implore thee to present at the throne of God,
that we may never fall into the snares
which are laid out for us,
and may all arrive at the port of salvation;
and, in so many dangers,

*may the Church and Christian society*
*sing once again the hymn of deliverance*
*and of victory and of peace. Amen.*

*In Thy conception, O Virgin Mary,*
*thou wast immaculate;*
*pray for us to the Father, whose Son,*
*Jesus Christ conceived of the Holy Spirit,*
*thou didst bring forth.*

*Mary encourages us
to reflect on Christ's life*

There are many good Christians who profess that they find it hard to pray. They keep God's commandments, they have a kind heart for their neighbor's distresses, and they are loyal to the Church, but they find no comfort or delight in prayer. Their prayers are dry, formal, and unconsoling. They are on the lips merely, not from the heart.

To be sure, a feeling of consolation is not the test of good prayer. Prayer is in the will — the yearning of the heart for God. A dry, comfortless prayer may be a very good one, because the will yearns mightily for God, despite the dryness of the feelings. Our feelings are neither meritorious nor wicked in the sight of God. What makes our merit or demerit is the motion of our free and lordly will. Our will is as a loud cry in the ears of God.

Yet it is a great help to have sweetness and consolation in prayer. It helps our will to move mightily, to yearn sincerely for God. In dryness and desolation, we crawl toward our goal with effort and sorrow. In consolation, we soar and fly, upborne on the wings of love. The wings of love! Love is the surest and swiftest aid to good praying. If we love well, we shall pray well. The two always walk hand in hand, and always help each other.

There are many motives for prayer: desire, when we yearn for some gift of God; fear, when we crave protection; penitence, when we beg pardon for our offenses. But of them all, the mightiest is love. "The lover flies, runs, and rejoices," says the *Imitation*. "He is free, and not held. He gives all for all, and has all in all, because he rests in one sovereign good above all, from whom all good flows and proceeds. . . . Love watches, and sleeping slumbers not. When weary, is not tired; when straitened, is not constrained; when frightened, is not disturbed, but, like a lively flame, and a torch all on fire, it mounts upward and securely passes through all opposition."[11]

[11] Thomas à Kempis, *Imitation of Christ*, Bk. 3, ch. 5.

# Mary encourages us to reflect on Christ's life

We must love well to pray well. What, then, is the surest way to love? To love our Lord well, we must know Him. How can we love what we do not know? The charm of the Godhead, the sweetness of His humanity, will irresistibly draw us to love, if only we know Jesus. But to know Him, we must study Him. We may know a great deal about Him, yet know Him very little. To love Him truly, we must know Him intimately; we must, as a modern poet has said, know Him by heart! Here, as in all the ways of Christian living, the Most Beloved Woman gives us a perfect example. She loved our Lord most perfectly, because she knew Him by heart.

⁀

## Mary pondered Christ in her heart

There is a single sentence in the Gospel of St. Luke that opens up for us tender vistas of comprehension of the love of Mary for Jesus. After the holy Evangelist has related the history of the birth of the Savior — that divine idyll saved in all its touching sweetness in the inspired word — he goes on to tell, "And all that heard wondered . . . at those things that were told them by the shepherds." Then, thinking of her from whose lips he had doubtless often heard the story of the Nativity, the holy writer adds, "But Mary kept all these words, pondering them in her heart."[12]

Here is the difference between hearing our Lord and truly knowing Him. "All that heard wondered." The Gospel story, which they heard from living witnesses, filled their minds with amazement, as it does our own when we read the words of the Scriptures, ages and ages afterward. But of these hearers of the good tidings, how many were stirred to active zeal and love of the newborn Savior? They heard and wondered, and went their way, and a thousand distracting interests and cares filled their hearts and crowded out the memory of the wondrous Birth. They wondered and forgot, as we have done many times after a sermon or a bit of reading that stirred our soul.

But not so the Most Beloved Woman. Most lovingly she kept all these words, pondering them in her heart. In the quiet days of Nazareth and Egypt, during the long, still mornings, when country peace fell all about her small cottage, and only the soft undertone of country sounds, the whir of insects, and the chatter of birds broke the drowsy silence, Mary was pondering in her heart the words that had to do with Jesus. Through the peaceful

[12] Luke 2:18-19.

afternoons, when she sat alone and sewed or spun under her quiet rooftree, her heart was dwelling on Him.

True, she had few of those trivial and plaguing distractions that keep our minds foolishly busy, away from God. The simple talk of her fellow villagers, a lowly and pious folk, whose thoughts ran soberly on betrothals and births and deaths, on crops and seasons and house-wifery, did not distract her thoughts from Him.

Now we are made restless with the chatter of many continents, and the low scandals of other nations crowd for space in the daily papers with the evil deeds at home.

But Mary's faith and devotion would have been proof even against the distractions of our shallow and noisy life. In any circumstances, with all her devoted might, she would have kept these words, pondering them in her heart. And as she pondered, her knowledge of her divine Son grew and widened and deepened in her heart. And with her knowledge grew her love!

*We should ponder the Scriptures*

If we wish to love Jesus, we must follow His Mother's example and ponder in our heart the words concerning Him. We have, in the New Testament, a portrait of His life and character, drawn by the Holy Spirit by the hands of the inspired writers. Christ's words, full of strength and sweetness, His deeds, showing forth the dignity of His Godhead, and the tenderness of His most perfect humanity are set down for us in language that everyone can understand. There are indeed mysteries in the Sacred Writ, and hard sayings. But on these we need not linger. Enough for us to read, with an open and humble mind, the clear, simple record of the life of Christ, from His birth to His death, and ponder it deeply in our hearts.

The Bible is a singular book among all the writings of men. To be understood, it must be read by the light of the grace of God. It gives up its sweet and tender secrets, not to the proud eye of the infidel and self-sufficient scholar, but to the lowly and pure of heart. The unbeliever may, and indeed does, study the sacred page and learn it by heart, with astonishing industry and skill. He sifts each word and peers into every grammatical construction. But he does not see Christ behind that maze of wordy criticism. Like dust blown into his eyes, the letter of the Scripture blinds him to its spirit and truth. He sees before him only a human document, amazingly old, intensely interesting, but merely human. No divine consolation flows to his heart from its pages. He does not see, in that sublime central Figure of all history, the dignity and sweetness of the Word-made-flesh.

It is the man or woman of lowly and simple faith, who yields humbly to the unerring teaching of Christ's Church, and follows her guidance through the Holy Scriptures, who best can understand the Heart of Christ as He has revealed it in the New Testament. If, therefore, you wish to know our Lord and so learn to love Him, follow the example of His Blessed Mother, and keep the words that tell of Him, humbly, pondering them in your heart. Keep always by you, where you can easily take it up at leisure moments, a copy of the Scriptures, and let your eyes drink in, often and even hourly, sweet sips of the inspired Word.

Then, pondering these things in your heart, you will grow into a blessed familiarity with Jesus. He will become for you an hourly memory, an intimate Presence, and a most consoling Friend. The thought of Him will color your whole life, as it did that of His Holy Mother, and while your mind dwells on the words concerning Him, your heart will often leap up to Him in spontaneous prayer. For we cannot truly know Jesus without loving Him, and prayer is the natural expression of our love.

❦

*Pondering Jesus sustained*
*Mary during her earthly life*

It was so with the Most Beloved Woman, our gentle model and guide in holy loving. The constant occupation of her days was to keep these words and ponder them in her heart.

From all sources she gathered the words of her Divine Son: from the disciples, who had shared His journeyings; from the holy women who followed Him about, ministering to Him; from the Apostles, who were His intimate friends. She had no need, indeed, to read them in the books of the Scriptures; the living word of the apostolic age was ever in her ears. She was the Mother of the infant Church and heard the Gospel story, in which she had borne so large a part, time and again from the very lips of the actors in it. Men's memories had not been spoiled, in that simple age, by the multiplication of trivial books. With a marvelous clearness of detail, they went over and over again all the memories of the life of Christ.

Tradition tells us that our Blessed Mother lived many years after the death of her Son. How could she endure to be separated from Him, whom she loved with so clinging and devoted a love? After the thirty years she had spent with Him, were not her days empty and full of longing, until she would once more see the light of His eyes and feel the touch of His hand in His everlasting kingdom? Was not earth an intolerable suffering of desire for her, and life an unbearable agony of expectation, until she would find once more Him whom she had lost?

We need not think so. This Child of her love and desire was with her still, in memory, hope, and love, although in His visible presence He had gone from her into Heaven. The words of Jesus still echoed in her ears with inconceivable sweetness. His looks still shone on her heart. St. John, the beloved, fed her upon the flesh of her Son in the Holy Eucharist, and still, faithful and devoted Virgin, she kept the words she had received, pondering them in her heart.

And thinking ever of Him and loving Him, she prayed to Him without ceasing, a mighty and continual prayer that pierced the heavens and moved the Heart of Christ and won unmeasured blessings for us all.

If, then, we wish to pray as she did, we must love as she did; and the way to that love she has likewise shown us: to learn our Lord by heart.

O Mary, you desire so much to see Jesus loved.
Since you love me, this is the favor that I ask of you:
to obtain for me a great personal love of Jesus Christ.
You obtain from your Son whatever you please;
pray, then, for me, that I may never lose the grace of God,
that I may increase in holiness and perfection from
day to day, and that I may faithfully and nobly
fulfill the great calling in life that
your Divine Son has given me.
By that grief which you suffered on Calvary,
when you beheld Jesus die on the Cross,
obtain for me a happy death,
that by loving Jesus and you,
my Mother, on earth, I may share your joy
in loving and blessing the Father, the Son,
and Holy Spirit forever in Heaven. Amen.[13]

[13] Prayer to Our Lady of Combermere. Used with permission of Madonna House, Combermere, Ontario.

*Mary reveals how to*
*make all our days holy*

God is sweetly merciful, even to the weaknesses and littleness of our souls. He understands this human nature, which He has made, supremely well. The secrets of our hearts lie utterly bare before Him, and He has planned His universe from all the ages to lead them powerfully back to Him. That is why in those sublime and most heroic examples that He puts before us, He has deigned to give us models of perfection even in little things.

Our lives, after all, are made up of little things. The great, eventful days are few and far between, and we look backward to them and forward, from the humdrum level of every day. Heroic opportunities, great occasions for stirring deeds, come to all of us only very rarely, and to most of us not at all. Our heroism, our sanctity, must spring from and be made out of the commonplace material of every day.

But our common, workaday lives seem so little fitted to be the soil of holiness! It seems to us so hard, even hopeless, to become true saints, great servants of God, in our present tedious surroundings. Our circumstances are so discouraging; our lot is so commonplace. We have such wearisome difficulties and temptations. Of course, we can struggle on with God's help and somehow save our souls. But any unusual holiness seems far beyond our powers in the grind and struggle of every day.

When we read some of the lives of the saints, they do not tend to encourage us. They describe the saints as beings so differently situated from us. Some of them were martyrs, and they had no choice but to be either saints or apostates. Others may seem to us to have been preternaturally shielded and protected in a holy life from their mother's arms. Still others performed penances or made acts of renunciation that are simply unthinkable for us. We cannot flee to deserts. We cannot spend our nights in prayer. Our weak bodies and weaker souls would break and shatter under such stress and struggle. They are hardly equal to the wear and worry of every day.

# Mary reveals how to make all our days holy

Again, to many sincere and earnest souls, great holiness seems such a complicated affair. To read some books on holiness, we would think the study of perfection was quite the most difficult study in the world. There are so many cautions and rules and admonitions. We must take so much thought and keep so many counsels. Busy, distracted men and women in the world — how can they hope to become holy? Is there no shortcut to saintliness? Is there no simpler means of sanctifying every day?

Of course there is. Hundreds and thousands of unlearned people, girls and boys, men and women, have found it out by God's grace, and are finding it out more and more in their humdrum workaday lives. The simple, obvious means that is making them more holy is the loving imitation of our Lord and His Blessed Mother.

Imitation is the easiest and most natural way of learning. Our minds and our bodies learn most readily and easily when we try to imitate what we see before us. From the little toddler who takes his first wobbly steps in the nursery, to the poet who writes an age-enduring epic, we all learn best and most quickly what we know by imitation. By imitating what is right and good, we are saved much trouble and speculation. There it is before us; we have only to put into practice what we see.

What a sweet mercy it is to us that God has given us for our imitation the two perfect characters of Jesus and Mary. For two thousand years, He taught and exhorted the Jews by their prophets and the patriarchs, and yet how dim and faint was their notion of holiness. Then Jesus and Mary, the Sun of holiness and the pure, luminous moon, beamed on the earth, and in one generation, the world was filled with saints and martyrs.

Again, think how alluring, how clear and easily understood is the example they offer us. They are not only the holiest; they are the most charming, lovable, and endearing of all the persons of history. The sweet, human attractiveness of their characters has made unbelievers sigh with admiration and delight. Our Lord and Savior is, indeed, the sublime and unique Model of all mankind. He combines in His own adorable yet human self all conceivable holiness and perfection. He is the supreme object lesson of sanctity and perfection. God became man to show mankind how to become like God.

*Mary shows us how to imitate Christ*

But the perfect sanctity of Mary brings out in dearest light the imitableness of Her divine Son. We might despair of following in the footsteps of God, but we see before us the gentle form of Mary. She, like us, was merely human. She, like us, was a mere creature, and yet she followed perfectly, in her own way, the perfect model of her Son. He is the source and exemplar of all holiness. She is His perfect follower and disciple. He shows us the supreme example. She points out to us the sweet and beautiful possibility of perfectly imitating Him. He leads us in the strait and narrow way. She encourages us, weak and human as we are, to walk behind Him in it.

Again, our dear Lord's character and mission might sometimes tend to obscure, to our weak eyes, the force of His example for us common men and women. He was the Lord's Anointed, the Priest and King of men. True, He spent thirty of His thirty-three years on earth, in giving us an example of the holiness of every day, of that humdrum and obscure and wearisome holiness that, as we have said, we common Christians find so difficult. Yet the three wonderful and superhuman years of the public ministry might make our feeble minds forget that lesson of the hidden life, if we did not have before our eyes a continual reminder in the sweet person of the Virgin Mary.

## A Marian Devotional

For all her life was a hidden life — a life devoted and consumed in the holiness of every day. How meekly and briefly this Most Beloved Woman appears, to our eager eyes, in the dear chronicle of the Gospels, how few were her public acts, how far between her public utterances. All her days passed in the small, outwardly insignificant occupations that take up so much of our waking hours. She practiced the sublime virtues and followed perfectly the perfect example of her Son, in the obscure, common, tedious duties of a housewife. The plainest of plain people, the unknown wife of a lowly carpenter, she was the Queen of Martyrs and Confessors, because she did little and obscure things, like our own daily actions, with more than a martyr's love and more than a confessor's faithfulness.

*We can attain holiness through*
*faithfulness to our daily tasks*

We excuse ourselves for not being holy by the plea that we cannot imitate the heroic excesses of the saints. Here is the Queen of Saints, the holiest of all mere creatures, and yet which one of us cannot follow in the footsteps of this lowly handmaid of God? She rose each morning to a day of simple, unseen toil like our own, a round of homely duties, of sweeping and dusting, cooking and spinning, in no way different from the work of the hundreds of thousands of Israel's daughters round about her. She did the work that servants and mothers of poor families do. But when she awakened to that day of toil, the flame of her heart rose straight toward God. For Him were every thought and word and action of hers simply intended, and with an inconceivable purity and intensity of love. He was the one sole Lord and Master of her heart.

We would be amazed, I think, if we could see the daily life of Jesus, Mary, and Joseph and would reflect that they were, of all creatures on earth, rendering the most heroic praise and service to God. Their life was as quiet and as uneventful as any day of ours could be. Prayer and work, work and prayer, the long, dull routine of uneventful mornings and afternoons, hard work for the Blessed Mother in her little cottage, hard work for Jesus and His foster father at the carpenter's bench — and all this for nearly twenty years! In this way, in these humdrum surroundings, these three lowly toilers gave God the supreme service, praise, and glory He had ever received or was ever to receive from all His human creatures.

How easy, then, it must be to be holy! How easy to imitate Jesus and His Most Beloved Mother: we can do so in any rank or employment whatsoever! Their holiness is sublime, yet it is most simple. It lies in the most absolute fidelity to the lowly, ordinary tasks of every day, from the motive of the most pure and constant love of God.

Do not undervalue, then, the holy opportunities that lie around you. It was from such opportunities that the Word Incarnate and His Virgin Mother built up their perfect holiness. When the heavens and the earth are no more, and the just exult forever in glory, their sweet converse together in eternity will not be of the great exploits of princes, nor even of the sublime austerities of the saints. They will more often look tenderly back on the little cottage of Nazareth, and their souls will overflow with sweetest rapture at the thought of the perfect, wonderful lives of that Holy Family, our blessed and heroic models of a perfect life of every day.

O most blessed and sweet Virgin Mary,
Mother of God, filled with all tenderness,
Daughter of the Most High King,
Lady of the Angels,
Mother of all the faithful,

On this day and all the days of my life,
I entrust to your merciful heart
my body and my soul,
all my acts, thoughts, choices,
desires, words, deeds,
my entire life and death,

So that, with your assistance,
all may be ordered to the good
according to the will of your beloved Son,
our Lord Jesus Christ.

From your beloved Son,
request for me the grace to resist firmly
the temptations of the world, the flesh, and the Devil.

My most holy Lady,
I also beseech you to obtain for me

true obedience and true humility of heart
So that I may recognize myself truly
as a sinner — wretched and weak —
and powerless, without the
grace and help of my Creator
and without your holy prayers.

Obtain for me as well,
O most sweet Lady,
true charity with which,
from the depths of my heart,
I may love your most holy Son,
our Lord Jesus Christ,
and, after Him,
love you above all other things.

Grant, O Queen of Heaven,
that ever in my heart
I may have fear and love alike
for your most sweet Son.

I pray also that, at the end of my life,
you, Mother without compare,
Gate of Heaven and Advocate of sinners,
will protect me with your great piety and mercy

*and obtain for me, through the blessed*
*and glorious Passion of your Son*
*and through your own intercession,*
*received in hope, the forgiveness of all my sins.*

*When I die in your love and His love,*
*may you direct me*
*into the way of salvation and blessedness. Amen.*

St. Thomas Aquinas[14]

[14] St. Thomas Aquinas (c. 1225-1274; Dominican philosopher, theologian, and Doctor), *The Aquinas Prayer Book,* ed. and trans. Robert Anderson and Johann Moser (Manchester, New Hampshire: Sophia Institute Press, 1999), 21.

## Mary teaches us how to love

We find it hard sometimes to reconcile the thought of supernatural love with natural affection. *Nature* is a word misused in so many ways that it has come at last to have an unpleasant sound. Not understanding that God's grace transforms and ennobles our natural affections, instead of supplanting and destroying them, too many persons come to think that there is some enmity between nature and grace, and that we must put off our tender and human affections in order to love God and man in a manner altogether supernatural and holy.

The cure for this illusion, as for so many others, is to look lovingly at the Most Beloved Woman. She is a sweetly perfect and intelligible compendium of practical holiness. She is a textbook of divine love; she is a perpetual object lesson to us, showing us in action the supernatural love of a mere creature for the Uncreated Love.

In the pure soul of Mary, nature and grace conspired together to enkindle her whole immaculate being with the sublime flame of heavenly love. The sweet and keen influence of God's grace, falling on her ready heart like pentecostal fire, transfigured all her mighty human affections and kindled them with supernatural love. Burning with God's fiery grace, her heart glowed utterly with unselfish love, and while her virginal mind dwelled perpetually on the Infinite Loveliness, her pure affections yearned for the God of Israel with unimaginable tenderness and power.

We must never forget that the heart of the Most Beloved Woman was in the truest, deepest sense a womanly heart. Man and woman, in the designs of God, are wonderfully meant to divide between them the activities of human life. Not only in the narrower sphere of wedlock, but in the broader family of the world, the man is ever meant to be the father; the woman is made to be a mother. Those good men and holy women who never take upon themselves the task of literal fatherhood or motherhood become by the very instinct of their hearts fathers and mothers to all around them. In the Church, by a holy felicity of phrase, priests are called "Fathers" and sisters are called "Mothers." The very hearts of good men and women lean toward and are made for the holy tenderness of a wide and spiritual fatherhood or motherhood.

The heart of our Blessed Lady was in the fullest, holiest sense a womanly heart. Her nature, unspoiled and perfect always as it came from the hands of God, was a womanly nature, tender, affectionate, and human. The womanly heart has a genius for love and devotion, and her divine Son had formed the heart of Mary to be a model for all loving hearts.

☙

*Mary directed all her love to God*

She had, then, by nature, a genius, so to speak, for loving, and the abounding grace of God and her own vigilant, steadfast will were ever ready to turn the whole power of that mighty love to its due object — God — and to her neighbor for God's love alone. Many men and women with great powers of self-devotion waste their love on unworthy objects; many sadly squander their hearts away. But the great heart of the Most

# A Marian Devotional

Beloved Woman poured all its splendid wealth of pure devotion with eager promptness at the feet of God. It needed the keen stroke of contrition to break the heart of Magdalene and pour her fragrant love at Jesus' feet.[15] But the virginal heart of Mary loved so from the beginning. Her love was as dutiful as it was sublime and mighty. Nature worked in her utterly with grace, and both together fanned her holy love.

These thoughts may in some way prepare us at least feebly to imagine how the Blessed Mother loved her adorable Son. The tiny virgin whose parents led her to the Temple had in her heart a flame of love for God, pure and fervent beyond what our faint hearts and dull intelligences can conceive. The growing maiden grew in love of God, and her strengthening powers were more and more enkindled with God's love. She loved Jehovah more than did even the fiery Isaiah, the pure Jeremiah, and the rapt Ezekiel. This little Jewish maid was a more valiant lover of her Lord than was David. She whispered the fiery love songs of the Prophet King and read into them more of fervor and tenderness than his great heart had comprehended. Already the little

[15] Cf. Luke 7:37 ff.

handmaid of the Lord had in her tender heart surpassed God's greatest lovers of old.

But the God whom Joseph's virginal spouse loved and adored was a hidden God, revealed only in dim prophecies and types and figures. True, she knew how to discern His lineaments in Creation and could mount the heights of contemplation and rise above all beauty and glory of creatures to the creating Majesty. But she began her life under the law of fear. It was her own Son who was to inaugurate the law of love!

Then, one day, in one supreme hour at which all other hours, past or to come, look forward or backward forever, the God whom her heart had always loved lay within her arms, her own Son! The Eternal had taken on Himself a life of moments and hours. The Infinite had come to lie within her slight, encircling arms. Now the great prophecies, the splendid types and figures on which her soul had dwelled for all her years, seemed pale and poor and dim beside this most glorious Reality. The center of all devotion lay on her own pure bosom. The tremendous, uncreated love, on whom her own love had fed and pondered, now spoke a near, sweet, intimate message to her, in the soft beatings of a little Heart!

Imagine, at that supreme moment, how Heaven and earth conspired together to multiply and deepen the love of the Most Beloved Woman. This God-Baby was all her own. Her whole nature, from which His human nature had sprung, yearned for Him with more than a mother's love. She was His only parent on earth, and whenever she looked upon Him, all the human tenderness of parenthood rose in sweet, overpowering fullness in her heart.

Most human and most heavenly — always most heavenly even when it was most deeply human — the love of Mary for Jesus is a shining lesson to us on how we may raise our human love to be divine. She would not have loved God well if she had not loved Him as His Mother. The love He had come to require of her was the love of a human mother, all transfigured and deepened and set on fire by the love of a creature for her God.

*We must love God and neighbor as Mary did*

In some such way, Jesus had come to every one of us, to demand from us a human love and tenderness. He will be loved, not only as our God, but also as our Brother, and He will have us love all our other brethren for His dear sake with pure and supernatural, and yet with tender and human, love. He bids us to keep in our hearts all kindliness, friendliness, and human charity, but to deepen and strengthen them with supernatural intent. We must love our elder Brother Jesus as Mary loved Him, and for His sake we must love ourselves and all mankind as Mary loved us for His sake.

Pray to the sweet Mother of God and of men that she may teach us the secret of her love, at once so human and so heavenly. Pray that we, in this unlovely and un-loving age, when there is so much talk of love and so lit-tle true, unselfish loving, may learn from her the secret of loving wisely and well both God and men. Ask her to make us comprehend how the deep possibilities of hu-man affection that we feel within us are not to be sup-pressed or stifled, but taught to borrow a divine and heavenly fire from God's ready grace, and to consume our hearts with tenderness for God and for our neigh-bor. She, the Most Beloved Woman, is also the Mother of fair love, and of fear, and of knowledge, and of holy hope.

*Immaculate Mother of God,*
*Queen of the Apostles,*
*we know that God's commandment of love*
*and our vocation to follow Jesus Christ*
*impels us to cooperate in the mission of the Church.*

*Realizing our own weakness,*
*we entrust the renewal of our personal lives*
*and our apostolate to your intercession.*

*We are confident that through God's mercy*
*and the infinite merits of Jesus Christ,*
*you, who are our Mother,*
*will obtain the strength of the Holy Spirit,*
*as you obtained it for the community of the Apostles*
*gathered in the upper room.*

*Therefore, relying on your maternal intercession,*
*we resolve from this moment to devote*
*our talents, learning, material resources,*
*our health, sickness and trials,*
*and every gift of nature and grace,*
*for the greater glory of God and the salvation of all.*
*We wish to carry on those activities which especially*

*promote the Catholic apostolate for the revival*
*of faith and love of the people of God*
*and so bring all men and women*
*into the Faith of Jesus Christ.*

*And if a time should come*
*when we have nothing more*
*to offer serviceable to this end,*
*we will never cease to pray that there will be*
*one fold and one shepherd, Jesus Christ.*

*In this way, we hope to enjoy*
*the results of the apostolate*
*of Jesus Christ for all eternity. Amen.*

St. Vincent Pallotti[16]

[16] St. Vincent Pallotti (1795-1850), pioneer of orga-
nized Catholic Action and founder of the Society of
Catholic Apostolate, also known as the Pallottini, or
Pallottine Fathers.

*Mary has exalted womanhood*

Jesus Christ, the eternal Son of God made man, has anointed and ennobled forever with the chrism of His Godhead our common humanity. It is a man and no angel or archangel, nor even one of the seraphim or the cherubim, who sits at the right hand of the Father and hears from Him those words, mysterious and sublime: "Thou art my Son; this day have I begotten Thee."[17]

For all the serene and blissful ages of eternity, we, with all the heavenly court and all the exalted princes of the nine choirs, shall adore, with that most profound homage which can be given to God alone, a Man, as truly man as He is truly God, as truly God as he is truly

[17] Ps. 2:7.

man — one of our race and our kind, a blood Brother of us all, now and for all eternity. The unction of the Godhead, the hypostatic union[18] has descended upon our humanity and given us a dignity and a standing in creation that, as some of the Fathers conjecture, stirred a third of the angelic host to envy and sent them hurling down in the fiery fall of their rebellion from Heaven to Hell rather than adore a God become man.

We are all sharers in this dignity. Although to only one human nature was it given to be assumed by the person of the Word so that it can be truly said that this is the body and the soul of God, still by that union we all are made blood brothers of the God-Man and become entitled to call ourselves with truth the kinsmen of the Son of God. More truly than the elevation of one of their race to earthly dignity confers nobility on all his kin, this substantial union of a body and a soul of our kind with the Word who is God confers on all the sons of Adam a nobility beyond human comprehension, which it will be the delight of Heaven to realize and which, even now, fills with ecstasy the saints and angels.

[18] That is, the union of the divine and human natures in the Person of Jesus Christ.

This consecration of our humanity extends marvelously to all the ordinary and commonplace actions of life that the Word-made-flesh has done for our instruction and salvation. Toil, which was for ages an ignoble thing, the penalty of the Fall and the compulsory occupation of slaves, is now ennobled, since the hands of Christ hewed wood and drew water and were busied for many days with labors.

Whatever God has touched is sanctified, and so food and sleep, the refreshment of conversation and the solitude of thought, the mart and the desert have become full of holy memories to him who sees Christ among the crowds or in the lonelinesses. Friendship, compassion, mercy, and justice have been sublimed and glorified because God has shown to us examples of these things. Nay, little human traits and emotions, weariness, trouble of soul, anxiety, and depression of spirit — He has sweetened and sanctified all these because He has suffered Himself to undergo them all for love of us and for our consolation.

This world is a different world, our humanity is changed and made sublime, and every human being is lifted to a new importance and dignity because God has walked on earth a man.

# A Marian Devotional

But there were certain relations of life that the God-made-man wished especially to consecrate and lift up in the esteem of the world for the good of all and for the carrying out of His merciful designs on humankind. The whole great and tender kingdom of womanhood as distinct from manhood, of the mother, the wife, the daughter, the cloistered virgin, and the woman in her home, needed pitifully to be lifted up from the contempt into which it had fallen and to be consecrated and given an example whereby all ages should be lit with the glory of a Christian womanhood no less than with a manhood after the model of Christ.

An awful degradation had fallen on the woman of pagan nations, and even among the chosen people of God, woman was held in small esteem, and her state called down the pity of the Most High. The Word-made-flesh took unto Himself the state and nature of a man. There was, then, need, so far as the design of the Most High may be said to have need of any creature, of a Woman who would give to women a model and an example that might interpret to them and convey to them that ennoblement and dignity of their state and nature which was theirs by reason of the Incarnation of the Word of God.

## Mary has exalted womanhood

*God gave Mary as a model for all women*

Looking with all-seeing and foreseeing wisdom down the ages, God found such a woman in the Virgin, our Mother Mary, and to her He assigned the most extreme honor, responsibility, and consecration that have been or ever shall be given to any mere creature. He anointed her in the counsels of the Godhead to be the Mother of the Word-made-flesh. She was to have, in her own person, all the supreme dignity that womanhood might gain from the mystery of the union of God with humanity. She was to be, in that sweet sentence never too often repeated, the Daughter of God the Father, the Mother of God the Son, and the Spouse of God the Holy Spirit. She was to remain forever a virgin, while becoming the Mother of the Most High, and was to unite, in her exalted humility, every resemblance of her divine Son, every unction of the Holy Spirit, every trait of faith, hope, love, and service to the Father that God Himself could desire in His Mother.

Most beloved of the Infinite Love, most encompassed by the cares of the Infinite Wisdom, most cherished in the counsels of the Father, this shining and spotless Virgin was to show to the world all the depths of holiness, the heights of dignity of womanhood, and by the unutterable sanctity of her consecration, she was to ennoble her whole sex and bring the selfish and stiff-necked race of men to bow in lowliness before a Mother holding her Child, a Virgin cherishing her Son.

Thenceforth, merely to know of the Virgin Mother Mary was to have in one's heart an epitome of the dignity, holiness, virtue, sweetness, and strength of womanhood as God Himself conceives it. For is it to be thought that Uncreated Wisdom, choosing from all eternity His own Mother according to the flesh, with His choice unbounded, and omnipotence and omniscience for His choosing, should have selected any but a woman who fulfills the very ideal of womanhood in God's mind?

In the Virgin Mother, then, behold the personal consecration of all womanhood forever, a woman who is the exemplar of her sex because she is so perfect and ideal a follower and image of Christ her Son, who is the Exemplar of mankind. Enthroned on the altars of the Church for all ages, written in her Liturgy, carved in her cathedrals, chanted in her hymns, and enshrined in the loftiest pages of her Doctors, theologians, and saints, behold the figure of a woman cherishing her Child. This masterpiece of God's own invention, this pinnacle of

mere creatures, this paragon of mankind is forever a con-
crete object lesson of the beauty and dignity of womanhood, a showing forth of the mind of God concerning
woman, a lesson of her majesty, an instruction of her
capabilities, a supreme example of her preciousness in
God's designs, a warning to her oppressors, a rebuke to
those who held her lightly, an everlasting consecration
of all that is holy, glorious, and powerful in woman, here
seen in its unique and wonderful extreme in her who
combines all the states and prerogatives of womanhood
in a way that it needed the ingenuity of the Most High
to conjecture and His omnipotence to bring to pass.

Maidenhood is forever consecrated in her who is
forever a maiden yet God's Mother. Motherhood is
sanctified in her who has the Infinite for a Son. Perpetual virginity has its best patron in her, the ever-virgin,
and she is besides the model of faithful spouses, keeping
the house of Joseph all the days of her married life with
an industry that was as perfect as her prayer. Contemplation and womanly reserve find their model in the
maiden of the Annunciation, when in the quiet prayer
of her own small room, she hears the message of an angel, and when her *fiat* draws down the Most High to be
her Son. The fearless courage of valiant women has the

inspiration of her example as she hastens through the mountain country to her cousin Elizabeth or walks near her agonized Son on the Way of the Cross. The grief of all mothers is summed up and consecrated in the sorrow of Mary standing in agony at the foot of the Cross; the joy of all motherhood is sanctified and sublimed in the joy of the Virgin Mother of Bethlehem whose curving arms enshrine the Desired of Ages.

Every age of womanhood is made lovely with pure and holy associations by the life of the Mother of God. Yonder little lass, with a face like a flower, tripping early to school, singing on her way, recalls the small Maid of Israel who went to be presented in the Temple. Her school days have sanctified the school days of all Christian girls; her fresh innocence has cast a holiness about the tender innocence of all children. The maiden

> "Standing, with reluctant feet,
>   Where the brook and river meet,
>   Womanhood and childhood fleet,"[19]

reminds us, in her rosy youth, of the Virgin of Judah, whose snowy purity and meek lowliness won the heart

---

[19] Henry Wadsworth Longfellow, "Maidenhood."

of the Most High to choose her for His virginal spouse. That most touching of human sights, a young mother with her baby, leaning over him to protect and cherish, or holding him in her encircling and sheltering arms, recalls most vividly the Mother and her Child. Even the declining years, when mothers see their sons depart or die and are left alone with memories, are sanctified by the recollection of the Mother of God, for the Fathers of the Church lead us to think that she dwelt with St. John at Ephesus until a ripe old age. The years left her virgin beauty untarnished who had no part of her own in that sin of which the punishment is old age and death; but still she bore all this long exile and separation from her sole Delight.

⌒

*Womanhood is lifted up in Mary*

Thus, Mary has gathered to herself all the loveliness of womanhood and left it tenfold more lovely by her consecrating memory. She has removed the stain and the reproach that dwelled with the name of woman since the Fall and restored to her sex that primacy of innocence, that light of honor which it was to have by nature and in the designs of God. She has rendered so sacred the innocence of maidens, the chastity of conse-crated virgins, the dignity of mothers, that, to those who know her and who love her, womanhood, so sorely outraged, so terribly degraded, has become the center of pure thoughts, the impulse to high devotion, the safe-guard against what is base, and the personification of what is chaste, tender, holy, and refined.

To realize what influence this single Woman has had upon the standing of her sex, consider for a moment what woman was in art, in literature, in family life, and before the law, during the ages that preceded the Chris-tian era. A jest, a plaything, a pretty trifle, the light and inconsequential possession of her father when she was young, of her master and husband when she grew ma-ture — this was the milder and the more endurable part of woman's lot.

Now consider woman as she is in Catholic art and letters, in the Christian home, and in the law that is in-spired and directed by Christian principles. There is one influence that has brought this liberation — the conse-cration of womanhood — to be, and that is the influ-ence of the Blessed Mother of God. With the Most Beloved Woman enthroned in Heaven and on earth, with the Mother of God offering her divine Child in her arms for the adoration of the ages, it is impossible for womankind to remain despised and degraded. She alone, by the soleness of her eminence, by the singleness of her glory, avails to lift up her whole sex and change the laughing contempt of pagan culture toward women into the reverential worship of Christian chivalry.

Over the whole world, over every age of the world, in all climes, and among all nations of the earth, there rises the image of a Woman carrying in her arms a Child. Around these two, inseparably united, shines a light most lovely and most human, yet not of this world but of Heaven. In the image of the Madonna, the dearest of all women, humanity and womanhood, freed from the primal curse and from the degradation of that first and most deadly sin of woman, the dignity of maiden, wife, and mother is consecrated and enthroned forever. As Christ gives to all mankind the dignity of being brothers and sisters of God, so Mary communicates to all women the glory of being sisters to God's Mother. In her, motherhood and maidenhood, the double crown of women, meet and are glorified. Is it not with justice that all generations cry out to that singular Virgin, "Blessed art thou among women"?

My soul magnifies the Lord,
and my spirit rejoices in God my Savior,
for He has regarded the low estate of His handmaiden.
For behold, henceforth all generations will call me blessed;
for He who is mighty has done great things for me,
and holy is His name.
And His mercy is on those who fear Him
from generation to generation.
He has shown strength with His arm,
He has scattered the proud in
the imagination of their hearts,
He has put down the mighty from their thrones
and exalted those of low degree;
He has filled the hungry with good things,
and the rich He has sent empty away.
He has helped His servant Israel,
in remembrance of His mercy,
as He spoke to our fathers,
to Abraham and to his posterity forever.[20]

[20] Luke 1:46-55 (Revised Standard Version).

## Mary leads us to God

There are two great ways of service by which a man or a woman may be of enduring benefit to our race: the service of word and the service of deed. Great words, moving words, that express the worthy aspirations of the heart of man, formulate his sublime desires, crystallize and keep in gleaming beauty and sparkling clearness his best and most glorious thoughts — such words are in themselves great deeds and form a permanent achievement, a lasting contribution to the riches of the soul and mind of man. To have uttered such words is a sublime service to humanity. They go echoing down the ages, crying forth from the dull covers of books, haunting human memories with thoughts of nobleness and power and enriching generations with their spiritual largess.

# A Marian Devotional

The eloquence of the soul, human heart speaking to human heart, knows no limits of space or time. A great word, once uttered and remembered, partakes of something of the undying youth of truth itself and survives, endures, leaps from mind to mind, from memory to memory for generation after generation.

Therefore the speakers of great words are honored among men with a singular reverence and gratitude. The prophets of old have the reverence of those who speak the hidden things of God. The Evangelists who uttered the great words that God gave them to utter have the honor of bringers of the Good Message. The Doctors of the Church, who, in their grand and simple way, gathered up and set forth in clear and moving human speech the mighty truths of the Church's treasury of revelation, are honored with special honor as speakers of the word. Even in profane letters, honor belongs to whom honor is due for the utterance of the age-long beauties and glories of perfect speech. The philosophers of old, Plato, Aristotle, the great poets, Homer and Hesiod, Sophocles, Euripides, the givers of excellent laws, Solon, Pericles, and all the long line of servers with the word, from that rosy dawn of Greek thought to our own day, Dante, Shakespeare, and their numerous company, have honor because they spoke greatly for the welfare of all aftertime.

But over and against this noble company of servers with the word, there are the servers with deeds, whose hearts and characters expressed in action have enriched all time. Some of them have been servers with words as well and have made afterdays resound as much with their speech as with the silent eloquence of their deeds. But all of them have spoken most convincingly by their actions, because if great words are a sort of deed, so, too, great deeds are a most powerful sort of word that cries down the years with a persuasive eloquence. Their actions are goodness made articulate, and their example speaks to our hearts with a conviction and persuasion that speech cannot come up to. When the past speaks stirringly to us, its voice is the sum of the great deeds we know of, the noble characters of old using either the direct language of words or the silent utterance of great deeds to move and inspire us.

Again, those who speak mightily to the ages often owe the strength of their inspiration to the deeds of those who have not spoken. The great authors from the beginning have gotten the power of their speech from the humanity about them and before them. They utter what many hearts have felt and many minds have thought before their own, and the grandeur of their conceptions is often borrowed from the deeds they have witnessed or have heard of before.

Thus, the service of deeds is mightier and more essential than that of words. Character has changed the course of ages and improved the world more than has eloquence or poetry. What we are avails more than what we say, and even the mightiest speech owes its influence and derives its power from deeds. Merely by being what they are and acting according to their heart and character, the greatest of men and women have made the world better and holier.

We see this very clearly in many characters of history, most clearly in the greatest character of all history: the Savior of the world. More than all other men together, He has served mankind by His words, for His teaching is indescribably precious and altogether necessary and indispensable to salvation. No other man ever spoke as this man, and the sum of His teaching is the New Testament of God to men, whether written in the Scriptures or kept in the Tradition of His Church. Yet His deeds are still more precious than His words, and His example speaks more movingly even than His teaching.

He is most eloquent when silent in Bethlehem, silent before His accusers, silent in the agony of the Passion, silent upon the Cross, where, with the eloquence of love and suffering, He speaks to sinners and to saints throughout all time.

☙

*Mary teaches us by word and by example*

It is so, too, with His Blessed Mother, the imitator of His perfect life. She, too, has served the world with words. The celestial hymning of the *Magnificat* rings everlasting, stirring the hearts of men, the sublime song of praise and exaltation, the supreme expression of humility and gratitude to God from the lips of the most exalted of mere creatures. It was she also who saved for all generations those precious incidents of the first dear days of her Son's life on earth, telling them to St. Luke so that he might embalm them in the clear amber of his Gospel, those words that she had kept in her heart: the coming of the angel, the going to visit and to minister to Elizabeth, the journey from Galilee, the birth of the Child and the laying in the manger, the shepherds and the Magi and the multitude of angels, the circumcision, the presentation, and that faring to Jerusalem when they lost the Boy and found Him again in the Temple. It was the mother's heart of Mary that kept all these words and gave them to the Evangelist for our everlasting comfort and delight. We would be pitifully poor of tidings of the precious early days, were it not for the kept words of Mary.

Still, her deeds were an unutterably greater service than her words. By being what she was, she has made all generations her debtors, and what she is speaks with far greater eloquence through the years than all she said.

We find some few famous women through the ages. Here and there in the story of nations, we come upon names of women honored greatly for what they have done for their people or for mankind. The Old Testament preserves the stories of women who rose gloriously to the call of duty or of opportunity and wrought heroic deeds or spoke undying words for God's chosen people. Judith was such a one; so also was the mother of the Maccabees, and Anna, the mother of Samuel, and Deborah, the prophetess, and Ruth and Esther. But these were rare exceptions to the common lot of women, which was obscure, lowly, and in subjection to the daily round of household cares.

So, too, in secular history we come upon some rare instances of great service rendered to the world by women, whether in word or in deed, but these, too, are the vast exception to that general rule which gave to men the leadership of the world and made it unlikely that even the greatest minds and the finest spirits among women would exert any widespread influence or achieve any notable service beyond the gentle sway that some Jewish women exerted at their own hearth and that politic dominion which the women of the Gentiles sometimes achieved by their intelligence or their charms.

Who, then, would have dreamed, surveying the past experience of mankind, that there would come into the world a woman who, by what she was and by the irresistible influence of her own personality and example, would more powerfully influence all afterages, more definitely change social ideas, break down bad customs, and implant great ideals than any individual in history, save only the Son of God Himself? Who could have conjectured that it would be a woman who would be second on the altars of the Church after God Incarnate, second in the hearts of the faithful after the Savior of the world, second in service and achievement after the supreme Benefactor of mankind, elevated above all other mere creatures, and loved and honored with a singular devotion, whom all generations should forever called blessed, not only for the gifts which the Most High had showered upon her, but also for the sublime service that she had used these gifts to render to God and man?

Singular proof of the wisdom of God and the folly of men! Astonishing and convincing instance of the power of example over words; of the excellence of the influence of goodness, the power of innocence and of love, of doing and being over the mere force of speech!

Among the great intelligences and strong wills of the ages, there has been a mighty strife for fame and for supremacy. Men, and women too, in immense numbers have spent weary lives striving for fame, for enduring influence, for the gratitude and the esteem of their fellowmen. The power of words and of deeds has been wooed and wrought upon to gratify the desire of these eager hearts for service and for honor. In lifelong planning, unremitting effort, and weariless desire, these men and women have built up the fabric of their fame and influence, only to see it wear weak with their declining years, crumble with death, and leave only a memory and a ruin for the pitiless centuries to make sport of and toss to dust. Out of the centuries rise mighty mausoleums, the last effort of kings to achieve undying influence and fame. The letters have crumbled from their inscriptions, and antiquaries come to wonder and conjecture in what age and among what nation this forgotten monarch lived.

Then, in a most obscure nation, among a despised and oppressed people, from a royal stock indeed, but fallen into poverty and oblivion, there is born a maiden on whom both earth and Heaven may well look with breathless expectancy. On her is put the loftiest responsibility, the most sublime office to be given in God's designs to any but His only-begotten Son made man. She is to render both to God and to men the greatest service asked of any except the Savior of mankind. Hers is a tremendous destiny and an opportunity at once unique and appalling. She is to be given graces beyond all other women, but heroic cooperation is required of her beyond what all other women must do and suffer. She will hear the voices of angels and hold to her breast the divine Child, but Simeon's sad prophecy will pierce her, and she must stand at last beneath the Cross, where her whole love and joy are crucified.

How did she achieve all that was set before her? How did she, a young maid, work out so perfectly all the vast designs of God and give to Heaven and earth a service unmatched by all women in all history? How did she come to a fame that is young and living, when all monarchies have fallen to dust, and that keeps her in the hearts and on the lips of men two thousand years after she has gone up into Heaven?

### Mary's humility has exalted her

The answer puts all human prudence to shame and justifies the ways of God. By entire humility, by complete confidence in God, by the perfect submission of her will in all things to His and the unending and unfathomable love that was the motive of all her actions, Mary, Mother of God, has surpassed in service and in honor all the great ones of old and the great ones still to be. God "hath regarded the humility of His handmaid, and behold from henceforth all generations shall call her blessed."[21]

Here is an immense consolation for all humble souls, a justification for those who renounce the great things of the world to serve Almighty God. Here is the wisdom

[21] Cf. Luke 1:48.

of God made manifest to men and the prudence of His counsels of self-renunciation, of meekness and lowliness of heart made clear in all their efficacy and power.

At the summit of service, first benefactor of the whole earth after her divine Son, stands the meek and lowly maiden of Israel whose whole life was passed in obscure labors and in hidden suffering and prayer. Her rare and precious words drift down the ages, repeated by the lips of the Evangelists of her divine Son, but not in these are her greatest praise and honor. All generations call her blessed for her humility, her love of God, her perfect conformity to His will, and her fidelity in those greatly important little things of life that, done well and with holiness, make great and perfect days.

At the summit of all mere creatures in dignity and in service, stands she who has epitomized all her character, her mission, and her greatness in the swift and perfect answer to the angel's message: "Behold the handmaid of the Lord."[22] Out of the mouth of the little ones has come wisdom. God has chosen the weak to confound the strong. The supreme praise and greatest reward of service have been achieved, not by lords in their might

---

[22] Luke 1:38.

nor sages in their ponderous wisdom, but by a little maid in a humble cottage, fulfilling perfectly the perfect will of God, herself a poem, a work of divine art, a deathless philosophy in action, the loveliest of copies of the love-liest and holiest of mankind, she who has ascended all Christian altars and been yet more dearly enshrined in all Christian hearts because her whole life was fidelity, love, and perfect service of God for His own sake and that of her fellows for the love of God.

Blessed Virgin Mary,
who can worthily repay you
with praise and thanks
for having rescued a fallen world
by your generous consent!

Receive our gratitude,
and by your prayers
obtain the pardon of our sins.
Take our prayers into the
sanctuary of Heaven, and enable them
to make our peace with God.

Holy Mary,
help the miserable,
strengthen the discouraged,
comfort the sorrowful,
pray for your people, plead for the clergy,
intercede for all women consecrated to God.

May all who venerate you
feel now your help and protection.
Be ready to help us when we pray,
and bring back to us the answers to our prayers.

*Make it your continual concern*
*to pray for the people of God,*
*for you were blessed by God*
*and were made worthy to bear*
*the Redeemer of the world,*
*who lives and reigns forever. Amen.*

St. Augustine of Hippo[23]

[23] St. Augustine (354-430), Bishop of Hippo.

## Mary is the perfect follower and reflection of Christ

"I am the way and the truth and the life," said our blessed Lord. "No man cometh to the Father but by me."[24] This saying shall stand until the end of time. There is one Exemplar of holy living given to the whole world, who is the Wisdom of the Father, having taken flesh to dwell among us and show us the path to God's justice and to His Heaven. There is one way in which all who wish to journey to everlasting glory must walk, one truth to which all who wish to possess the uncreated Truth in His fullness forever must hold, one life whereby all who will have life eternal in the mansions of His

[24] John 14:6.

Father must live. No man, no one of all the race of Adam comes to the Father in earthly justice or in heavenly glory save through His only-begotten Son, who is made flesh, so that all flesh may see salvation.

Our perfection, then, lies in following the simple and lovely precept to imitate and follow the example of the Son of God. Perfection, which puzzled in its elusive pursuit the most profound of pre-Christian philosophers, which perplexed in its details even the holy men of Israel before the coming of Christ, is now made visible, sensible, and easy of comprehension to even the simplest of us all.

The Word has become flesh and has walked among us. Men and women like ourselves have seen Perfection in the flesh, have walked with Him, spoken with Him, and watched with immense eagerness and faithful memory His words and deeds, and they have handed down to us such exact teachings, such clear precepts and precise examples from Him that the perfection which He taught, most certain and secure because it is of God Himself, most imitable because it is given by one of our own flesh and blood, is put, so to speak, into our hands, and we can see and feel what God would have us imitate for our salvation and for His glory.

# Mary is the perfect follower of Christ

Yet our human weakness, given a model so perfect yet so appealing, so utterly conformed to the holiness of God and yet so perfectly suited to our human condition, desires yet one thing more to help us to follow Him. We desire not only to see Him whom we are to imitate but to be shown how to imitate Him. We yearn to be convinced, not that He is to be followed — for that we have on God's own word and our hearts' witness saying to us, "Come, let us follow Him" — but that it is truly in our personal power to follow Him closely. He walks before us and is perfect, but we wish to see some mere creatures like ourselves following perfectly after Him. Nothing gives us more courage and confidence in walking in His footsteps than to see others of our own flesh and blood following after the Word-made-flesh.

⁓

## Mary shows us how to follow Christ

God, therefore, in His pity and kindness, knowing that we need to be shown how to follow, as well as to be shown the way, has raised up for us all one entirely perfect follower of His Son. One instance has been given us of a mere creature like ourselves who has most worthily and fully followed the way, possessed the truth, achieved the life, and come in all the fullness of grace and glory to the Father through the Son whom He has sent. In this consummate follower of Christ, this perfect imitator of the perfect Exemplar, we have a guide and an encourager who can show us how Christ is to be imitated and demonstrate to us that it is not beyond the power of our human nature, helped by God's grace, to walk in the way, achieve the truth, and possess the life in all the fullness that God desires.

To us all, therefore, the Virgin Mother is the supreme encourager and guide in the perfect imitation of her Son. Her example is full of reassurance for us, her very image reminds us of Him of whom she herself is the living image. Being a mere creature like us, she made herself so like unto the Son of God that even were she not His Mother, she would still remind us of none but Him and of Him most perfectly by her extreme resemblance to Him. Most children take after and resemble in some sort their mother. This Mother takes after, and resembles in a marvelously perfect way, her Child.

One mere human being has, then, achieved the most perfect resemblance to the Word-made-flesh, and although we can never hope in this life to come so near to Him as does His immaculate Mother, still the very fact that she has so perfectly and gloriously succeeded is of good omen to us and makes us hope that in our kind and our degree we also shall achieve a glorious likeness to Him.

### Mary is particularly an example for women

But it is to womankind in particular that the Most Beloved Woman is supremely a benefactor in showing them how to imitate her divine and perfect Son. For the Word chose according to the will of His Father to become a man, and, perfect in all things, He is in all things full of a holy and Godlike manliness. His ways are the ways of a man; His thought, His speech, His manner of acting, the spirit and method of His teaching, and the works of His public life all bear the firm imprint of a manly character.

Now, it has been well observed that in the character of every fine and noble man, there is something of the woman, and that in every noble and perfect woman, there is something of the man. The one has the delicacy of feeling, the fineness of nature that is characteristic of women; the other has the strength of purpose, the steadiness of will that we are accustomed to associate with men. This is true, but the very comparison points also to great differences between the sexes. The manly and the womanly nature are designed by Almighty God to supplement and complement each other, and so there are essential and radical dissimilarities between them. Men are strong, and women are tender. Men are bold, women yielding and retiring. Men find their most congenial sphere of action in public life, in the rush of affairs, in struggle and effort; women, with rare exceptions, long for more peaceful ways, prefer the quiet of a home, shrink from overmuch stress and conflict, are happiest when they are ministering to children and the elderly, not fighting for place or pushing a cause.

In most things, then, the terms we apply to men and to women are not quite univocal; their virtues and their qualities are not precisely of the same temper and the same meaning. Courage in a woman means a different thing, although not a less glorious thing, than in a man. So also does affection, sympathy, devotion, strength, wisdom, prudence, and generosity. It is true that in other things, in purity, faith, and charity, they are on equal terms. But we look for traits of womanliness that would be out of place and sometimes unbecoming in a manly character, and for touches of manliness that would be strange and out of place in the character of a perfect woman.

So, although Christ's example is as much for women as for men and His sublime teaching strikes to the tender heart of the maiden as surely as to the strong heart of a man, it was a merciful and considerate condescension to the special exigencies of womanhood that God should give to all women a model so entirely their own. In this exalted Woman, chosen and approved by God Himself and full of the excellencies peculiar to their sex, and at the same time so perfectly an image of the Word-made-flesh, they have at once a guide and model, so that they may see, as it were, at a glance how to imitate the Man-God completely while at the same time keeping completely within the meet sphere of their womanhood.

⌒

*Mary reflects Christ's light*

A poet says neatly, although not quite truly, "Woman is the lesser man, and all thy passions, match'd with mine / Are as moonlight unto sunlight, and as water unto wine."[25] It is the saying of a man for the moment

[25] Alfred Lord Tennyson, "Locksley Hall."

out of patience with womankind and seeking to bring out the difference between the heart of man and of woman in a bitter figure, which makes the heart of woman not only different from, but inferior to, that of man.

Because she is milder, gentler, and more tender by nature and in feeling, woman is not therefore less strong and noble than man. Hers is a subjection that brings her rule, a lowliness and service that implies control. "As unto the bow the cord is / So unto the man is woman. Though she bends him she obeys him / Though she draws him yet she follows. . . ."[26]

All controversies, therefore, concerning the superiority of either sex should come to rest at last in the simple truth that manhood and womanhood, in nature, in intelligence, and in the qualities of heart and of soul, are neither inferior nor superior to the other, although nature gives to men an eminence of strength, the headship of the family, and therefore a greater dignity.

Yet when we speak of our Lord and His Blessed Mother, this comparison of the poet, stripped of its bitter meaning, becomes luminous and lovely. Many a

---

[26] Henry Wadsworth Longfellow, "The Song of Hiawatha," Pt. 10.

devout worshiper of the Mother of God has dwelled delighted upon her virtues under the image of the moon, which gives back with a changed and gentle luster the mighty radiance of the sun. Travelers in southern climates love to tell of the brightness, the clear and silver beauty of the moon in those limpid skies. Swimming large in the heavens, the tropic moon pours on the earth such a torrent of white radiance that the world becomes visible again almost as at midday, but it is a different and transfigured world. The bright colors of day are softened to silver; the firm outlines of midday are touched with the dimness and vagueness of the dawn.

In some such way does the fair Mirror of the Word give to the world the very light of her Son, but softened to the silvery radiance of the heart and soul of woman. It is His very light, the pure and unchanged ray of the Light who enlightens every man that comes into this world,[27] but it is reflected from the mind, the will, the feelings, and the emotions of the most perfect and womanly of all women, who thus interprets to her sex all the fair teaching of her Son and shows them a world of thought, feeling, and action, a sphere of willing

[27] John 1:9.

suffering and doing, which is the same world indeed that is made manifest by the Sun of Justice, but with its colors softened to their conception and its outlines traced for the comprehension of their hearts.

Thus, the Christian ideal has two perfect models: the one, the great original of all holiness and justice, who is God Himself made man and walking among us so that we may see and hear and understand from the example of a God in what the perfection and dignity of our human nature consist; the other by the most perfect imitator and follower of Christ, who at the same time gives to all mankind the lesson of how He is to be followed and interprets for her own sex the Christian character. Jesus is the Source of Light, the True Light that enlightens the world, and Mary, the consummate Mirror of the Light, who sheds upon the world the selfsame ray, caught in the bosom of a mere creature like ourselves and poured forth again unimpaired.

When the sun has set, and the skies purple with dusk, the moon swims to sight in the East like a new sun of the night and rises to the noon of midnight, giving to the world a memory and a trace of the light that is concealed. But again, when it is day, who has not seen the moon hiding itself in the brightness of the heavens, a pale watcher and rejoicer in the brilliance of that sun from whom it has borrowed all its beams?

So, too, the Most Beloved Woman, borrowing all her light from her Beloved, shines on us to remind us of the true Light of the World, and then conceals herself in the brightness of the Source and Wellspring of her splendor. So, too, does she shine forth for the glory of all womankind, giving to the earth a gleaming and convincing proof of the majesty of womanhood and to her sex a light and guide to the imitation of her Son. Then she hastens to lose and hide herself in the radiance of His light, the watcher of and rejoicer in the sole and singular glory of Him who is the way, the truth, and the life for all ages to man and woman, Jew and Gentile, bond and free.

O Jesus, Divine Master,
I thank and bless Your most merciful Heart
for having given us Mary most holy
as our Mother, Teacher, and Queen.
From the Cross You placed us all in her hands.
You gave her a great heart, much
wisdom, and immense power.
May all mankind know her, and pray for her!
May all permit themselves to be led by her
to You, the Savior of mankind!
I placed myself in her hands,
as You placed Yourself.
With this Mother I want to live now,
in the hour of my death,
and for all eternity. Amen.

*Edward F. Garesché, S.J.*

(1876-1960)

Born in St. Louis, Missouri, Edward Francis Garesché attended St. Louis University and Washington University and practiced law for two years before entering the Jesuit novitiate in Florrisant, Missouri. He was ordained a priest in 1912.

Fr. Garesché's priesthood was devoted to medical mission work and saw a vast literary output. He wrote seven volumes of poetry, for which he is best known, as well as twenty-four books, ten booklets, and numerous articles on subjects as diverse as prayer, meditation, inspiration, art, history, science, the teachings of the saints, sodality, education, pastoral theology, and nursing.

# A Marian Devotional

He founded *The Queen's Work*, a magazine of the Sodality of the Blessed Virgin, and edited *Hospital Progress and Medical Mission News*, a publication of the Catholic Medical Mission Board, of which he was president and director. Fr. Garesché also established the Knights of the Blessed Sacrament in the United States, began a Catholic Young Men's Association, and served as the spiritual director of the International Committee of the Catholic Federation of Nurses and of the Daughters of Mary, Health of the Sick.

Drawing on his wide-ranging interests and experience and with clear, inspiring words, Fr. Garesché offers his readers practical wisdom on how to find true success in life — that is, the attainment of holiness and happiness through good citizenship, prudent choices, and dutiful service to God and to others.

*⌒*

## Sophia Institute Press®

Sophia Institute™ is a nonprofit institution that seeks to restore man's knowledge of eternal truth, including man's knowledge of his own nature, his relation to other persons, and his relation to God. Sophia Institute Press® serves this end in numerous ways: it publishes translations of foreign works to make them accessible to English-speaking readers; it brings out-of-print books back into print; and it publishes important new books that fulfill the ideals of Sophia Institute™. These books afford readers a rich source of the enduring wisdom of mankind.

Sophia Institute Press® makes these high-quality books available to the general public by using advanced technology and by soliciting donations to subsidize its general publishing costs. Your generosity can help Sophia

Institute Press® to provide the public with editions of works containing the enduring wisdom of the ages. Please send your tax-deductible contribution to the address below. We also welcome your questions, comments, and suggestions.

*For your free catalog, call:*
**Toll-free: 1-800-888-9344**

*or write:*
Sophia Institute Press®
Box 5284
Manchester, NH 03108

*or visit our website:*
www.sophiainstitute.com

Sophia Institute™ is a tax-exempt institution
as defined by the Internal Revenue Code,
Section 501(c)(3). Tax I.D. 22-2548708.